RESEARCH BIBLIOGRAPHIES & CHECKLISTS

30

A Gil Vicente Bibliography

RESEARCH BIBLIOGRAPHIES & CHECKLISTS

R̶C̶B

General Editors

A.D. Deyermond, J.R. Little and J.E. Varey

A GIL VICENTE BIBLIOGRAPHY
(1940-1975)

by

CONSTANTINE C. STATHATOS

with a Preface
by
Thomas R. Hart

Grant & Cutler Ltd
1980

© Grant & Cutler Ltd

1980

ISBN 0 7293 0089 7

I.S.B.N. 84-499-4869-X

DEPÓSITO LEGAL: V. 1.840 - 1981

Printed in Spain by Artes Gráficas Soler, S.A., Valencia

for

GRANT & CUTLER LTD

11, BUCKINGHAM STREET, LONDON, W.C.2.

Στή μνήμη τοῦ πατέρα μου, Χριστοφόρου,

καί τοῦ I.S. Révah, πατέρα τῶν Βισεντινῶν σπουδῶν

CONTENTS

PREFACE

Bruce W. Wardropper has sketched the formation of a canon of critical studies on the Spanish theatre of the Golden Age.[1] He argues persuasively that "the greatest gain in our apprehension of this theatre came about in the 1930s when some English Hispanists— E. M. Wilson, A. A. Parker, W. J. Entwistle, and a few others—began to read Calderón with the critical methods that had been developed by T.S. Eliot, I.A. Richards, and F.R. Leavis" (p. 177). Wardropper suggests that their success with Calderón is due in part to the special qualities of his theatre, which "lends itself particularly to this kind of intellectual close reading". The plays of Lope de Vega, on the other hand, "do not easily yield their secrets to a criticism dealing with ideas and artistic structure. If Lope was a thinker, he was not a systematic thinker; if he was an artist, he did not so much construct his plays as allow them to find their own form". For Wardropper, Lope's "serious theatre is a dramatic weaving of essentially lyric themes . . . . It follows that those critical methods which yield the best results when applied to a sonnet or an eclogue are the ones that need to be used in order to analyze one of his plays" (p. 179). Wardropper asserts that "we understand well only one work by Lope, his *Fuenteovejuna*. This is because, by tacit consent, a number of critics converged on this play over a prolonged period of time, until it surrendered its mystery".

I have cited Wardropper's discussion of Lope at such length because I believe that much of it is applicable to the theatre of Gil Vicente. There are, of course, great differences between Vicente and Lope. Dámaso Alonso has contrasted Vicente's handling of plot and character in *Don Duardos* with the way Lope and his followers dealt with similar materials (no. 301).[2] But surely the similarities are also apparent. In particular, the importance of the

---

[1] "The Criticism of the Spanish *Comedia*: *El caballero de Olmedo* as Object Lesson", *Philological Quarterly*, LI (1972), 177-96.

[2] Numbers in parentheses refer to items in the *Bibliography*.

lyric elements in Vicente's theatre may help to explain why his plays have often fared so well in the hands of critics known primarily for their work on lyric poetry; first and foremost Dámaso Alonso, of course, but also Leo Spitzer and Elias Rivers. Though Wardropper is doubtless best known for his work on the *comedia*, he has also written extensively and well about the poetry of the *siglo de oro*; characteristically, his contribution to Vicente studies is an examination of the way imagery contributes to what he calls "the metaphysical sense" of *Don Duardos* and *Amadís de Gaula* (no. 636).

The role played by studies of *Fuenteovejuna* (and, I should add, of *Peribáñez*) in shaping our understanding of Lope's theatre corresponds to that played by studies of *Don Duardos* (nos 301, 636, 742) and of the *Auto de la sibila Casandra* (nos 329, 368, 710, 711) in shaping our understanding of Vicente's. For most of Vicente's other plays there is not even one such study. Indeed, for most of the Portuguese and bilingual works we do not have even a reliable edition, certainly not an annotated edition that would make them accessible to students—and, it may be added, attractive to scholars who are not specialists in sixteenth-century Portuguese literature. The last point is of particular importance. Every student of Vicente owes a debt of gratitude to the handful of scholars who have made him their central concern: Eugenio Asensio, Stephen Reckert, Paul Teyssier, the late I. S. Révah, to name only some of the more recent. But the organization of Hispanic studies both in Spain and in the English-speaking world makes it possible for very few people to devote themselves exclusively or even primarily to Portuguese literature. In looking through Professor Stathatos' admirable bibliography, one is struck by how many fundamental contributions to our understanding of Vicente have come from scholars who have written about no other Portuguese author.

If the uniqueness of Vicente's achievement has attracted the attention of scholars who are not specialists in Portuguese, it may also have caused some Hispanists to give him rather less than his due. It is a commonplace to say that much of his work represents a road not taken by the later Portuguese—or Spanish—theatre. Critical insights derived from the study of the later *comedia*—both that of Lope and that of Calderón—are not always immediately useful in understanding his work. We do not yet know precisely what questions we should ask as we approach the texts of his plays, especially perhaps those that T. P. Waldron (no. 141) has called allegorical fantasies, such plays as the *Comédia sobre a divisa da cidade de Coimbra* or *Floresta de enganos*. Clearly, much remains to be done and Professor Stathatos' bibliography is to be welcomed because it helps to ease some of the difficulties that stand in the way of doing it.

One of those difficulties surely is the reluctance of many students of Spanish literature to embark on the study of a Portuguese writer. One reason for this reluctance is, of course, that so many of Vicente's plays are written wholly or partly in Portuguese, but I believe that there is another and perhaps more important reason. Almost everyone who has attempted to do research on Vicente must have become uncomfortably aware that the resources of most university libraries, both in Britain and in America, are apt to be limited—certainly far more limited than for a Castilian writer of comparable importance. Professor Stathatos' bibliography enables students of Vicente's theatre to use those limited resources more efficiently. While many of the books he lists will be found only in the largest university libraries, his lists of reviews, many in easily accessible journals not primarily devoted to Portuguese studies will often make it possible to get an idea of a book's content and to decide whether it is important enough—and close enough to the subject of one's own research—to justify the trouble of obtaining a copy from another library. Reviews, moreover, sometimes contain important statements by distinguished authorities (e.g. no. 88.1, in which Marcel Bataillon assesses Révah's account of the roles played by the Inquisition and by Vicente's son Luis in the publication of the *Copilaçam* of 1562). Again, it is sometimes helpful to know that an important article has been published in more than one place. Thus, two major studies by Eugenio Asensio, one first published in the *Anais do Primeiro Congresso Brasileiro de Língua Falada no Teatro* and the other in the excellent but short-lived *Bulletin d'Histoire du Théâtre Portugais*, may now be read in his *Estudios portugueses* (no. 303), while a student who does not read German may be glad to know that some articles of Albin Beau first published in that language may now be read in Portuguese (no. 306).

Professor Stathatos' bibliography includes a number of references to Vicente in works primarily concerned with other matters which may escape the attention of a *vicentista*, especially one new to the field (e.g. nos 322, 336). Finally, his bibliography makes it easy to tell which aspects of Vicente's theatre have so far received little or no scholarly attention. These are by no means always the least interesting, and Professor Stathatos has performed a real service to scholarship by helping us see more clearly the gaps in our knowledge of one of the most rewarding writers in Hispanic literature.

Thomas R. Hart

INTRODUCTION

The obvious conclusion to be drawn from a glance at the large output of Vicentine scholarship in the last thirty-five years is that international interest in Gil Vicente has been growing fast. As a result, long-standing attitudes which tended to focus on the achievements of Gil Vicente, the voice of *portugalidade*, at the expense of Gil Vicente, the artist, have been losing ground. New facets of his artistry are constantly brought to light and established critical clichés are questioned and reassessed. Yet much still remains to be done in this area.

In order that their task be facilitated and their interest in Gil Vicente enhanced, Vicentists should be provided with a few very basic but at the same time indispensable tools, namely, a greater number of reliable critical texts, a concordance of the dramatist's complete works, a cumulative glossary elucidating his idiom, and, finally, a register of Vicentine scholarship.

It is the last-named need that the present work seeks, albeit modestly, to satisfy. Since the most significant work on Gil Vicente has been produced in the last two or three decades, the bibliography compiled by Luísa Maria de Castro e Azevedo (1942) has lost part of its usefulness. The catalogues of pertinent holdings of the University of Coimbra and the public libraries of Oporto, Santarém, and Évora, issued in 1965 on the occasion of the fifth centenary of Gil Vicente's birth (see entry no. B24), leave much to be desired. With the possible exception of the checklist issued by the Municipal Library of Santarém, the information provided is more often than not inadequate. Furthermore, in addition to being very limited, all four lists are composed almost exclusively of Portuguese contributions.

Some of the effects of the lack of a comprehensive bibliography can be seen in the few instances in which some scholars have followed a certain line of inquiry unaware, presumably, of retracing someone else's steps. The present work was conceived as a remedy.

My task did not prove to be an easy one, as I had to surmount several obstacles, the major one of which was the inaccessibility of a large number of Portuguese journals even within Portugal. A lesser but equally frustrating difficulty was provided by the fact that in Portugal, as perhaps elsewhere in the Hispanic world, it is not unusual for an article to appear in several journals at the same or at different times, with or without revision (there have been cases of one article appearing, in exactly the same form, four times in journals and books).

Considering that selectivity tends at times to fall victim to arbitrariness, I set completeness as my goal, although it became clear in the process that completeness in an area like this can be rather elusive (especially in the case of book reviews). Any indication, therefore, of possible omissions or oversights will be greatly appreciated.

This bibliography comprises those contributions to the study of Gil Vicente which appeared between 1940 and 1975. One important post-1975 item has been included (Stephen Reckert's *Gil Vicente: espíritu y letra*, 285A), since it makes available in a single volume the author's earlier work in revised and expanded form. More recent book reviews are also included. Pre-1940 items can be found in Luísa Maria de Castro e Azevedo's *Bibliografia vicentina* (see entry no. B19). Works which originally appeared before 1940 have been listed, if they were reprinted or reedited since that year.

The body of this work is divided into three main parts: editions and adaptations, translations, and critical studies. Entries in Part I have been arranged chronologically (by date of publication in Sections A, B, D) rather than alphabetically, unless two or more editions appeared in the same year. Section C is similarly arranged by date of composition or performance, as the case may be, of each play, in accordance with the dates proposed by the late I. S. Révah (see entry no. 451). The listing in Part II is alphabetical (by language). So is the arrangement in the first three sections of Part III, whereas Section Di is categorized thematically. These categories are too broad to be watertight, and there are some items which might have been listed under other headings. If the thematic breakdown appears somewhat arbitrary, it was judged to be more convenient and useful than a mere alphabetical listing of all articles. Finally, Section Dii follows the same pattern as Section C of Part I. Asterisked items have not been seen by the compiler.

It is hoped that this compilation proves to be satisfactory and useful in the continuing study of Gil Vicente.

Parts of this work have appeared or are due to appear in the following journals:

'Editions and Adaptations of Gil Vicente's Works (1940-1975)', *Segismundo*, 23-24 (1976), 87-110.
'A Bibliography of Translations of Gil Vicente's Works Since 1940', *Vórtice*, I, 3 (1975 copyright by the Board of Trustees of the Leland Stanford Junior University), 83-88.
'French Contributions to the Study of Gil Vicente: A Bibliography (1942-1975)', *Luso-Brazilian Review*, XV (1978 copyright by the Board of Regents of the University of Wisconsin System), 105-16.
'Germanic Contributions to the Study of Gil Vicente Since 1940: A Bibliography', *Iberoromania* (in press).
'Anglo-American Contributions to the Study of Gil Vicente: A Bibliography (1940-1975)', *Sillages*, 5 (1977), 127-56.
'Italian Contributions to the Study of Gil Vicente since 1942: A Bibliography', *Sillages*, 6 (in press).

My debt to other bibliographies is indicated in the section on bibliographic sources. Here I wish to extend my thanks to the University of Wisconsin-Parkside for a summer grant which enabled me to do some research in the Biblioteca Nacional de Lisboa, and to the staff of the Wisconsin Interlibrary Loan Service for their patience and cooperation. Thanks also go to Professors A. D. Deyermond and J. E. Varey for their close critical reading of the manuscript and their numerous suggestions.

C. C. S.
University of Wisconsin-Parkside

ABBREVIATIONS

AHSI　　*Archivum Historicum Societatis Iesu* (Roma)

AION-SR　*Annali dell'Istituto Universitario Orientale-Sezione Romanza* (Napoli)

Anon.　　Anonymous

ASNSL　*Archiv für das Studium der Neueren Sprachen und Literaturen* (Braunschweig)

BAbr　　*Books Abroad*. A Quarterly Publication Devoted to Articles on Foreign Literatures and Reviews of Foreign Books (Norman, Oklahoma)

BCom　　*Bulletin of the Comediantes* (Los Angeles)

BdF　　　*Boletim de Filologia* (Lisboa)

BEP　　　*Bulletin des Études Portugaises et de l'Institut Français au Portugal* (Coimbra)

BGPL　　*Boletim do Gabinete Português de Leitura* (Pôrto Alegre)

BH　　　　*Bulletin Hispanique*. Annales de la Faculté des Lettres de Bordeaux (Bordeaux)

BHS　　　*Bulletin of Hispanic Studies* (Liverpool). [*Bulletin of Spanish Studies* up to 1949]

BHTP　　*Bulletin d'Histoire du Théâtre Portugais* (Lisboa, 1950-1954)

BMSLP　*Boletim Mensal da Sociedade de Língua Portuguesa*. A Bem da Língua Portuguesa (Lisboa)

CH　　　　*Cuadernos Hispanoamericanos*. Revista Mensual de Cultura Hispánica (Madrid)

Ch.　　　Chapter

CN　　　　*Cultura Neolatina*. Bollettino dell'Istituto di Filologia Romanza (Roma)

CoL　　　*Colóquio/Letras* (Lisboa). [Previously *Colóquio*]

col., cols　column (s)

ComP　　*O Comércio do Porto* (Porto)

comp.　　compiler (s), compiled by

CSIC   Consejo Superior de Investigaciones Científicas

DA(I)   *Dissertation Abstracts* (Ann Arbor, Michigan) [*International* begin-
            ning with XXX (1969-70), no. 1]

dir.   director, directed by

ed.   edition, editor(s), edited by

EIP   *Estudos Italianos em Portugal* (Lisboa)

ELit   *Estafeta Literaria.* Revista Quincenal de Libros, Artes y Espec-
            táculos (Madrid)

ESPSL   *O Estado de São Paulo. Suplemento Literário* (São Paulo)

EUDEBA   Editorial Universitaria de Buenos Aires

GilV   *Gil Vicente.* Revista de Portugalidade (Guimarães)

HR   *Hispanic Review.* A Quarterly Journal Devoted to Research in the
            Hispanic Languages and Literatures (Philadelphia)

illus.   illustrator, illustrated by

JAULLA   *Journal of the Australasian Universities Language and Literature
            Association* (Christchurch, New Zealand)

L-BR   *Luso-Brazilian Review* (Madison, Wisconsin)

LGRP   *Litteraturblatt für Germanischen und Romanischen Philologie*
            (Leipzig)

LR   *Les Lettres Romanes* (Louvain)

MLJ   *Modern Language Journal* (Boulder, Colorado)

MLN   *Modern Language Notes* (Baltimore)

MLR   *Modern Language Review.* A Quarterly Journal Devoted to the
            Study of Medieval and Modern Literature and Philology (Cambridge)

MPhi   *Modern Philology* (Chicago)

n.d.   no date

NGui   *Notícias de Guimarães* (Guimarães)

no., nos   number (s)

NRFH   *Nueva Revista de Filología Hispánica* (México, D.F.)

PP   *Philologica Pragensia.* Academia Scientiarum Bohemoslovenica
            (Praha)

PRJ   *O Primeiro de Janeiro* (Porto)

PUF   Presses Universitaires de France

QIA   *Quaderni Ibero-Americani.* Associazione per i Rapporti Culturali
            con la Spagna, il Portogallo e l'America Latina (Torino)

RdH	*Revista de História.* Sociedade Portuguesa de Estudos Históricos (Lisboa)
RdL	*Revista de Literatura* (Madrid)
RdP	*Revista de Portugal* (Lisboa)
rev.	revised
RF	*Romanische Forschungen.* Vierteljahrschrift für Romanische Sprachen und Literaturen (Erlangen)
RFE	*Revista de Filología Española* (Madrid)
RFH	*Revista de Filología Hispánica* (Buenos Aires, 1939-1946)　　[Superseded by the *Nueva Revista de Filología Hispánica*]
RFLUL	*Revista da Faculdade de Letras da Universidade de Lisboa* (Lisboa)
RHM	*Revista Hispánica Moderna* (New York)
RHTh	*Revue d'Histoire du Théâtre.* Publication de la Société d'Histoire du Théâtre (Paris)
RJ	*Romanistisches Jahrbuch* (Hamburg)
RLR	*Revue des Langues Romanes* (Montpellier)
RomN	*Romance Notes* (Chapel Hill, North Carolina)
RPF	*Revista Portuguesa de Filologia* (Coimbra)
RPhi	*Romance Philology* (Berkeley)
RR	*Romanic Review.* A Quarterly Publication of the Department of Romance Languages in Columbia University (New York)
StN	*Studia Neophilologica* (Uppsala)
TeM	*O Tempo e o Modo.* Revista de Pensamento e Acção (Lisboa)
TLS	*Times Literary Supplement* (London)
trans.	translation, translator (s), translated by
VKR	*Volkstum und Kultur der Romanen* (Hamburg)
vol., vols	volume (s)
ZRP	*Zeitschrift für Romanische Philologie* (Halle, Tübingen)

BIBLIOGRAPHIC SOURCES

I Periodical

B1   *Boletim de Bibliografia Portuguesa.* Lisboa, Biblioteca Nacional.

B2   *Boletim Internacional de Bibliografia Luso-Brasileira.* Lisboa, Fundação Calouste Gulbenkian. I (1960) -XIV (1973).

B3   *Bulletin of the Comediantes.* Los Angeles ('A Current Bibliography of Foreign Publications Dealing with the *comedia*'). From II (1950), no. 2 on.

B4   *Dissertation Abstracts.* Ann Arbor, Michigan. [' ... *International*' beginning with XXX (1969-70), no. 1]

B5   *Hispania.* American Association of Teachers of Spanish and Portuguese. Wichita, Kansas ('Dissertations in the Hispanic Languages and Literatures').

B6   *MLA International Bibliography of Books and Articles on the Modern Languages and Literatures.* Modern Language Association of America. New York. [*MLA American Bibliography* ... until 1956]

B7   *Modern Language Journal.* Boulder, Colorado ('American Doctoral Degrees Granted in the Field of Modern Languages').

B8   *Nueva Revista de Filología Hispánica.* México ('Bibliografía').

B9   *Revista de Filología Española.* Madrid ('Bibliografía').

B10   *Revista de Literatura.* Madrid ('Información bibliográfica').

B11   *Revista Portuguesa de Filologia.* Coimbra ('Notas bibliográficas'). I (1947)-.

B12   *Revue d'Histoire du Théâtre.* Paris ('Bibliographie'). I (1948)-.

B13   *Studies in Philology.* Chapel Hill, North Carolina ('Recent Literature of the Renaissance: A Bibliography and Index'). Through LXVI (1969).

B14   *The Year's Work in Modern Language Studies.* Modern Humanities Research Association. Cambridge.

B15   *Zeitschrift für Romanische Philologie. Bibliographie.* Halle, Tübingen. [*Romanische Bibliographie/Bibliographie Romane/Romance Bibliography* since 1965]

II Other

B16   Anon. 'Bibliografia [vicentina].' *Dionysos*, X, 12 (September 1965), 60-1.

B17 Anon. 'Tesis doctorales de interés literario de la Universidad de Madrid.' *RdL*, XXI (1962), 107-16.

B18 Azevedo Filho, Leodegário A. de. 'A edição crítica de textos portugueses.' *Ocidente*, LXXXIII (1972), 90-100.

B19 Azevedo, Luísa Maria de Castro e. *Bibliografia vicentina.* Lisboa: Biblioteca Nacional, 1942. xii + 1002 pp.
   Reviews:
   .1. A.J. da Costa Pimpão, *Biblos*, XIX (1943), 578-81.
   .2. Domingos Maurício, *Brotéria*, XXXVII (1943), 470.
   .3. Manoel da S.S. Cardozo, *BAbr*, XIX (1945), 202.

B20 Bleznick, Donald W. *A Sourcebook for Hispanic Literature and Language: A Selected, Annotated Guide to Spanish and Spanish American Bibliography, Literature, Linguistics, Journals, and Other Source Materials.* Philadelphia: Temple University Press, 1974. xi + 183 pp.

B21 *Catalog of Luso-Brazilian Material in the University of New Mexico Libraries.* Ed. Theresa Gillett &Helen McIntyre. Metuchen, N.J.: Scarecrow Press, 1970. 961 pp.

B22 *A Catalogue of the Greenlee Collection. The Newberry Library, Chicago.* Boston: G.K. Hall, 1970. 2 vols.
   See also below, no. B54.

B23 Chatham, James R. & Enrique Ruiz-Fornells. *Dissertations in Hispanic Languages and Literatures: An Index of Dissertations Completed in the United States and Canada (1876-1966).* Lexington: The University Press of Kentucky, 1970. xiv + 120 pp.

B24 Comissão Nacional do V Centenário de Gil Vicente. *Exposições vicentinas. Catálogo.* Lisboa: Ministério da Educação Nacional, 1965. 143 pp.
   Contents: Biblioteca Geral da Universidade de Coimbra. Biblioteca Pública Municipal do Porto. Biblioteca Municipal de Santarém. Biblioteca Pública de Évora.

B25 Dolci, Giulio. 'Gil Vicente na língua italiana.' *Boletim Cultural da Câmara Municipal do Porto*, XX (1958), 292-8.

B26 Estorninho, Carlos. 'Portuguese Literature in English Translation.' In *Portugal and Brazil: An Introduction. Made by Friends of Edgar Prestage and Aubrey Fitz Gerald Bell in piam memoriam.* Ed. H.V. Livermore. Oxford: Clarendon Press, 1963, pp. 129-38.

B27 Grismer, Raymond L. *Bibliography of the Drama of Spain and Spanish America.* 2 vols. Minneapolis, Minnesota: Burgess-Beckwith, [1967-9]. 231, 231 pp.

B28 *Guía para la consulta de la "Revista de Filología Española" (1914-1960).*

Comp. Alice M. Pollin & Raquel Kersten. New York: New York University Press, 1964. 835 pp.

B29 Hodcroft, F. W. 'Theses in Hispanic Studies Approved for Higher Degrees in British and Irish Universities (1972-1974).' *BHS*, LII (1975), 325-44.

B30 Jiménez, Pedro. 'Información de Bélgica: tesis sobre temas hispánicos presentadas en las universidades de Bélgica (1964-1971).' *Boletín de Filología Española*, XIV-XV (1974-5), 35-7.

B31 Jones, C. A. 'Theses in Hispanic Studies Approved for Higher Degrees by British Universities to 1971.' *BHS*, XLIX (1972), 325-54.
    Items dating from 1913.

B32 *The Literatures of the World in English Translation: A Bibliography*. III: *The Romance Literatures, Part I*. Ed. George B. Parks & Ruth Z. Temple. New York: Ungar, 1970. 473 pp.

B33 McCready, Warren T. *Bibliografía temática de estudios sobre el teatro español antiguo (1850-1950)*. Toronto: University of Toronto Press, 1966. xix + 445 pp.
    Reviews:
    .1. H.W. Hilborn, *Canadian Modern Language Review,* XXIII (1966), 61-2.
    .2. J. Manuel Rozas, *Segismundo*, III (1967), 393-400.
    .3. Carlos Ortigoza, *Hispanic American Historical Review*, XLVIII (1968), 688-9.
    .4. Rafael Osuna, *Thesaurus*, XXIII (1968), 587-90.
    .5. Richard W. Tyler, *MPhi*, LXV (1967-8), 246-7.
    .6. Walter Poesse, *HR*, XXXVII (1969), 414-17.
    .7. N.D. Shergold, *BHS*, XLVI (1969), 86-7.
    .8. Luis Alberto Luna Tobar, *Archivum Bibliographicum Carmelitanum*, XII (1970), 204.
    .9. Charlotte Stern, *RPhi*, XXIX (1975-6), 135-7.

B34 Moisés, Massaud. *Bibliografia da literatura portuguêsa*. São Paulo: Saraiva Editora da Universidade de São Paulo, 1968. 383 pp.
    Review:
    .1. Gerald M. Moser, *Hispania*, LIII (1970), 326-7.

B35 Moser, Gerald M. 'Portuguese Literature in Recent Years.' *MLJ:*
    1945-7: XXXII (1948), 581-8.
    1948-50: XXXV (1951), 455-63.
    1951-3: XXXVIII (1954), 347-53.
    1954-6: XLI (1957), 183-93.
    1957-9: XLIV (1960), 245-54; XLV (1961), 59-60.
    1960-1: XLVI (1962), 289-92; XLVII (1963), 238-42.
    1962-5: L (1966), 483-92.

B36 ——. 'Recent Publications on Portuguese Language and Literature (1945-1947).' *Hispania*, XXXI (1948), 163-74, 387-97.

B37 O'Brien, Robert Alfred. *Spanish Plays in English Translation: An Annotated Bibliography*. New York: Las Américas, 1963. 70 pp.

B38 Paci, Anna Maria. *Manual de bibliografía española*. Pisa: Università, 1970. 828 pp.
　　Review:
　　.1. H.B. Hall, *BHS*, LIV (1977), 84-5.

B39 Pane, Remigio Ugo. *English Translations from the Spanish (1484-1943): A Bibliography*. New Brunswick, N.J.: Rutgers University Press, 1944. vi + 218 pp.

B40 *Portugal e o Brasil: catálogo de livros portugueses e brasileiros e publicações estrangeiras sobre Portugal e o Brasil editado pela Biblioteca da Universidade de Utrecht em colaboração com o Instituto de Estudos Hispânicos, Portugueses e Ibero-Americanos da Universidade de Utrecht.* 3 vols. Utrecht, 1959, 1962, 1966. 403, 326, 382 pp.

B41 Reis, J.E. Morgado. 'Supplément à la "Bibliographie des travaux sur l'histoire du théâtre portugais parus de 1947 à 1950".' *BHTP*, II (1951), 255-9.

B42 Révah, I.S. 'Bibliographie des travaux sur l'histoire du théâtre portugais parus de 1947 à 1950.' *BHTP*, II (1951), 107-12.

B43 Rodríguez Richart, José. '*Habilitationsschriften* y tesis de doctorado realizadas en las universidades de Austria, de la República Democrática Alemana y de la República Federal de Alemania, sobre temas de lengua y literatura española y portuguesa (1945-1974).' *Iberoromania*, new series, 3 (1975), 205-25.

B44 Rogers, Francis M. &David T. Haberly. *Brazil, Portugal and Other Portuguese-speaking Lands: A List of Books Primarily in English*. Cambridge, Mass.: Harvard University Press, 1968. 73 pp.

B45 Rudder, Robert S. *The Literature of Spain in English Translation: A Bibliography*. New York: Ungar, 1975. ix + 637 pp.
　　Reviews:
　　.1. J.J. Troiano, *Library Journal*, C (1975), 1813.
　　.2. Anon., *Choice*, XII (1975-6), 1294.
　　.3. Anon., *Booklist*, LXXII (1976), 1425.
　　.4. John Crow, *Hispania*, LIX (1976), 544.
　　.5. H.C. Woodbridge, *MLJ*, LX (1976), 78-9.
　　.6. David Mackenzie, *BHS*, LIV (1977), 233.

B46 Serís, Homero. *Manual de bibliografía de la literatura española.* 2 parts. Syracuse, N.Y.: Centro de Estudios Hispánicos, 1948-54. xliii + 1086 pp.

B47 Sheren, Paul. *The Portuguese and Brazilian Theatre*. Romsey, Hants.: Motley Books, 1974. xxix + 94 pp.
Annotated checklist. Includes an introductory bibliographical survey of Gil Vicente's life and works (pp. iii-viii).

B48 Simón Díaz, José. *Manual de bibliografía de la literatura española*. Segunda edición ampliada con unas adiciones (1962-1964, 1965-1970). Barcelona: Gustavo Gili, 1971. vii + 603 + 100 + 198 pp.
Reviews: (of the first ed., 1963):
.1. Juan Manuel Rozas, *RFE*, XLVI (1963), 490-3.
.2. Rafael María de Hornedo, *Razón y Fe*, 805 (February 1965), 210.
.3. Warren T. McCready, *HR*, XXXIII (1965), 395-9.
.4. Frank Pierce, *BHS*, XLII (1965), 278.
.5. H.C. Woodbridge, *Hispania*, XLVIII (1965), 610.

B49 Sletsjøe, Leif. 'Les Études portugaises dans les pays scandinaves.' In *Actes du Quatrième Congrès des Romanistes Scandinaves publiés à l'occasion du soixantième anniversaire de Holger Sten*. Copenhague: Akademisk Forlag, 1967, pp. 163-79.
See also below, no. B51.

B50 —. 'Los estudios vicentinos.' *CH*, 280-2 (October-December 1973), 378-84.

B51 —. 'Os estudos portugueses nos países escandinavos.' *Colóquio*, 53 (April 1969), 61-3.

B52 Stathatos, Constantine C. 'A Bibliography of Translations of Gil Vicente's Works since 1940.' *Vórtice*, I, 3 (Autumn 1975), 83-8.

B53 Tavani, Giuseppe. 'I più recenti studi italiani sulla letteratura portoghese medievale.' *Anuario de Estudios Medievales*, III (1966), 565-73.
'Gil Vicente e il teatro medievale,' pp. 570-3.

B54 Welsh, Doris Varner. *A Catalog of the William B. Greenlee Collection of Portuguese History and Literature and the Portuguese Materials in the Newberry Library*. Chicago: Newberry Library, 1953. viii + 342 pp.
Reviews:
.1. I.S. Révah, *BEP*, XVIII (1954), 205.
.2. B.M. Woodbridge, *RPhi*, IX (1955-6), 472.

B55 See also below, no. 398, pp. 215-18.

EDITIONS AND ADAPTATIONS

A. Complete Works

1 *Obras completas.* Ed. Marques Braga. 6 vols. Lisboa: Sá da Costa, 1942-4. (Subsequent reprints)
   Reviews:
   .1. Calvert J. Winter, *BAbr*, XVIII (1944), 92 [on vol. II], 300 [on vol.I].
   .2. Consuelo Howatt, *BAbr*, XIX (1945), 94 [on vols III & IV].
   .3. M. Muñoz Cortés, *RFE*, XXIX (1945), 366.
   .4. Aubrey F.G. Bell, *BAbr*, XX (1946), 85-6 [on vol. VI].

2 *Obras completas.* 2 vols. São Paulo: Edições Cultura, 1946. 552, 613 pp. No mention of an editor nor of editorial procedure. Vol. I: Obras de devaçám, comédias, tragicomédias (*Dom Duardos* only); Vol. II: tragicomédias, farsas, obras miúdas (in these last is included a selection of 29 lyrics, pp. 591-607).

3 *Obras completas.* Ed. Álvaro Júlio da Costa Pimpão. Illus. Joaquim Lopes. New revised ed. Porto: Livraria Civilização, 1962. lxxxiii + 602 pp. (First ed.: Barcelos: Editora do Minho, 1956)

4 *Obras completas: autos, farsas, comédias, tragicomédias, obras várias. Contribuições para o conhecimento das obras de Gil Vicente.* Porto: Lello & Irmão, 1965. vi + 1468 pp.
   Review:
   .1. A.R , *Brotéria*, LXXXI (1965), 711.

5 *Obras completas. Edição comemorativa do V centenário do nascimento de Gil Vicente.* Ed. Reis Brasil [José Gomes Bras]. Published so far:
   Vol. I. Lisboa: Minerva, 1966. 237 pp.
      (*Visitação, Auto pastoril castelhano, Auto dos Reis Magos, Auto da sibila Cassandra, Auto de São Martinho, Quem tem farelos?*)
      Review:
      .1. G.S., *Brotéria*, LXXXIV (1967), 560.
   Vol. II. Lisboa: Livraria Portugal, 1968. 272 pp.
      (*Sermão, Auto da Índia, Auto da Fé, Auto das fadas, Auto dos Quatro Tempos*)
   Vol. III. Lisboa: Livraria Portugal, 1970. 241 pp.
      (*Velho da horta, Exortação da guerra, Comédia do viúvo*)

B. *Collections and anthologies*

  i. Drama

6   *Obras. Estudo com transcrições de tôda a obra vicentina, e as peças completas da Exhortação da guerra, Auto da Alma, Côrtes de Júpiter, Inez Pereira e Quem tem farelos?*. Ed. Arlindo de Sousa. Porto: Livraria Civilização, 1940. 374 pp.

7   Mendes, Fonseca. *Contos de mestre Gil inspirados na obra de Gil Vicente (narrativas infantis)*. Lisboa: Globo, 1941. 136 pp.

8.   Braamcamp Freire, Anselmo. *Vida e obras de Gil Vicente "trovador, mestre da Balança"*. 2nd revised ed. Lisboa: Revista Ocidente, 1944. Includes the texts of the *Pranto de Maria Parda* (Palha copy and 1562) and of *Inês Pereira* (Madrid copy and 1562) on pp. 465-73 and 473-98 respectively.

9   Révah, I.S. *Deux "autos" méconnus de Gil Vicente. Première édition moderne*. Lisbonne: Ottosgráfica, 1948. 92 pp.
    (*Obra da geração humana* and *Auto de Deus Padre e Justiça e Misericórdia*. See also below, no. 286)
    Reviews:
     .1. A.J. da Costa Pimpão, *Biblos*, XXIV (1948), 571-4.
     .2. Eugenio Asensio, *RFE*, XXXIII (1949), 409-14.
     .3. Georges Le Gentil, *BH*, LI (1949), 63-7.
     .4. A.J. Saraiva, *Portucale*, XXII (1949), 277-80.
     .5. Marcel Bataillon, *RPhi*, III (1949-50), 319-22.
     .6. Aubrey F.G. Bell, *BAbr*, XXIV (1950), 47; and *HR*, XVIII (1950), 348-50.
     .7. Joseph E. Gillet, *RR*, XLI (1950), 216-18.
     .8. U.T. Holmes, *Hispania*, XXXIII (1950), 182-3.
     .9. A.R. Nykl, *MLN*, LXV (1950), 275-6.
     .10. Robert Ricard, *RHTh*, II (1950), 94-5.
     .11. Gomes de Zurara, *Brotéria*, L (1950), 591-2.

10   *Dois autos de Gil Vicente: "Mofina Mendes" e "Auto da Alma"*. Ed. Sousa da Silveira. Rio de Janeiro: Centro de Estudos de Língua Portuguesa, 1949. 78 pp.
    Also: Rio de Janeiro: Simões, 1953, and Ministério da Educação e Cultura, 1973.

11   *Excertos de Gil Vicente e Camões*. Ed. Eduardo Pinheiro. Porto: Livraria Simões Lopes, 1949. 258 pp.

12   *Presépio vicentino (história do Natal para ser contada e representada)*. Ed. Joaquim de Oliveira. Vila do Conde: Gráfica de Santa Clara, 1956. 78 pp. (Also: Lisboa: Bertrand, 1957)

12A *Antología mayor de la literatura española*. II: *Renacimiento (Siglo XVI)*.
Thesaurus Litterae: Antologías Labor de la Literatura Universal: España,
II. Ed. Guillermo Díaz-Plaja. Barcelona: Labor, 1958, pp. 376-94. 2nd
ed., 1969.
Selections from *Sibila Casandra, Auto da Barca da Glória, Comédia do
viúvo*. Names of collaborators are given but it is not clear who prepared
each section of the volume.

12B *Las mejores escenas del teatro español e hispanoamericano (desde sus
orígenes hasta la época actual)*. Ed. **Antonio** Espina. Madrid: Aguilar,
1959, pp. 44-9.
Selections from *Dom Duardos*.

13 *Teatro de Gil Vicente*. Ed. António José Saraiva. Lisboa: Portugália,
1959. 396 pp.
Also 1963, 1967, 1968. In addition to abridged texts, it includes the
complete versions of *Quem tem farelos?, Auto da Barca do Inferno,
Auto da Alma, Auto da Inês Pereira, Auto da feira*.
Review:
.1. F.S., *Ocidente*, LVII (1959), 223.

14 *Os autos das Barcas*. Ed. Augusto César Pires de Lima. Porto: Domingos
Barreira, 1960. 202 pp.

15 *Auto de Mofina Mendes. Diálogo infantil da "Comédia de Rubena"*.
Ed. António A. Machado de Vilhena. Porto: Domingos Barreira, 1962.
136 pp.
Review:
.1. J.P. Machado, *RdP*, XXVIII (1963),400-2.

16 *Obras dramáticas castellanas* Ed. Thomas R. Hart. Clásicos Castellanos,
CLVI. Madrid: Espasa-Calpe, 1962. lxi + 278 pp.
2nd ed., 1968. *Auto de la visitación, Auto pastoril castellano, Auto de
los Reyes Magos, Auto de San Martín, Auto de la sibila Casandra, Auto
de los cuatro Tiempos, Auto de la Barca de la Gloria, Comedia del viudo,
Tragicomedia de Don Duardos, Auto de las gitanas, Tragicomedia de
Amadís de Gaula*.
Reviews:
.1. J.P. Machado, *RdP*, XXVIII (1963), 114.
.2. Gerald Moser, *Hispania*, XLVI (1963), 170-1.
.3. Charlotte Stern, *HR*, XXXII (1964), 164-9.
.4. J.E. Tomlins, *MLN*, LXXIX (1964), 561-4.
.5. A.L.-F. Askins, *RPhi*, XVIII (1964-5), 521-2.
.6. Leif Sletsjøe, *StN*, XXXVIII (1966), 136-9.
.7. P. Heugas, *BH*, LXXVI (1974), 228-9.

17 'Fragmentos vicentinos.' *Vértice*, XXV (1965), 825-30. Excerpts from
several plays.

18 *O velho da horta. Auto da Barca do Inferno. Farsa de Inês Pereira.* Ed. Segismundo Spina. São Paulo: Brasiliense, 1965. xxxviii + 134 pp. (4th ed., 1970)

19 *Pequena introdução às obras de Gil Vicente.* Ed. Arlindo de Sousa. Porto: Progresso, 1965. 290 pp.

20 *Gil Vicente e as crianças. Prefácio de Paulo Quintela. Textos selecionados por Maria Leonor de Carvalhão Buescu.* Lisboa: Ministério da Educação Nacional, 1966. 36 pp.

21 Gomes, Torquato. *Auto das lamentações e queixas de Gil Vicente, recolhidas e ordenadas por um admirador obscuro durante as comemorações do seu quinto centenário.* Braga: Livraria Cruz, 1966. 52 pp.

22 *Presença da literatura portuguêsa. História e antologia.* I: *Era medieval.* Ed. Segismundo Spina. 2nd revised ed. São Paulo: Difusão Européia do Livro, 1966, pp. 156-80. (3rd ed., 1969)

23 *Roteiro literário do Brasil e de Portugal: antologia da língua portuguêsa.* Ed. Álvaro Lins & Aurélio Buarque de Hollanda. Vol. I. 2nd rev. ed. Rio de Janeiro: Civilização Brasileira, 1966, pp. 35-42.
Excerpts from *Mofina Mendes, Auto da feira* and *Barca do Purgatório.*

24 *Autos das três Barcas.* Lisboa: Estúdios Cor, 1967.
Facsimile edition.

25 *Antologia arcaica. Trechos em prosa e verso, coligidos em obras do século VIII ao século XVI.* Ed. Francisco da Silveira Bueno. 2nd ed. São Paulo: Saraiva, 1968, pp. 182-93.
Excerpts from the *Auto da cananeia* and *O velho da horta.*

26 *Four plays.* Ed. & trans. Aubrey F.G. Bell. New York: Kraus Reprint Co., 1969. li + 98 pp.
Reprint of the 1920 ed. (Cambridge: University Press). Contains the following texts accompanied by verse translations: *Auto da Alma, Exhortação da guerra, Farsa dos almocreves, Tragicomédia pastoril da Serra da Estrela.* The bilingual edition of the *Auto da Alma* appeared first in *MLR*, XIII (1918), 58-77.
Review:
.1. George Young, *MLR*, XVI (1921), 186-7.

27 *Obras-primas do teatro vicentino.* Ed. Segismundo Spina. São Paulo: Difusão Européia do Livro, 1970. 329 pp.
O velho da horta, Quem tem farelos?, Auto de Mofina Mendes, Auto da Barca do Inferno, Auto da Alma, Farsa de Inês Pereira, Auto da feira, Farsa dos almocreves, Romagem de agravados, Auto da Lusitânia.

28 *Antologia do teatro de Gil Vicente.* Ed. Cleonice Berardinelli. Rio de Janeiro: Grifo, 1971. 398 pp.

Contains, in addition to excerpts, the complete texts of the following: *Auto da Alma, Auto da feira, Breve sumário da história de Deus, Auto da Barca do Inferno, Auto de Inês Pereira, Farsa chamada Auto da Índia, Auto de "Quem tem farelos?"*, "Carta de Gil Vicente ao Rei D. João III, sôbre o sermão que pregou aos frades de Santarém" (pp. 359-64).

29 *Farces and Festival Plays.* Ed. Thomas R. Hart. Eugene: University of Oregon Books, 1972. 234 pp.
    Auto da Índia, Quem tem farelos?, Frágua de Amor, Côrtes de Júpiter, O triunfo do Inverno.
    Reviews:
    .1. C.C. Stathatos, *L–BR*, X (1973), 272-4.
    .2. John Brotherton, *JAULLA*, 41 (1974), 132-3.
    .3. T.F. Earle, *MLR*, LXIX(1974), 900.
    .4. John Lihani, *Hispania*, LVII (1974), 596-7.
    .5. Helmut Siepmann, *RF*, LXXXVI (1974), 219-22.
    .6. Roger M. Walker, *Comparative Literature*, XXVI (1974), 282-4.
    .7. Alice R. Clemente, *MPhi*, LXXII (1974-5), 294-6.
    .8. Charlotte Stern, *HR*, XLIII (1975), 82-5.

30 Moisés, Massaud. *A literatura portuguêsa através dos textos.* 5th revised ed. São Paulo: Cultrix, 1972. 527 pp.
    Includes the text of the scene of Todo o Mundo e Ninguém (*Auto da Lusitânia*) with commentary.

31 *Autos de Gil Vicente.* Ed. Cleonice Berardinelli. Rio de Janeiro: Agir, 1974. 136 pp.
    Includes the complete text of *Inês Pereira* (pp. 19-66), an almost complete version of the *Auto da feira* (pp. 67-100), and selections from *Mofina Mendes, Auto da Alma, Auto da Barca do Purgatório, Auto da Lusitânia.*

32 *Os autos das Barcas.* Fixação do texto, introducão, notas e tradução do terceiro auto de Luiz Francisco Rebello. 2nd ed. Lisboa: Europa-América, 1975. 145 pp.
    Inferno (pp. 27-61); *Purgatório* (pp. 63-90); *Glória* (pp. 91-120).

32A *Sátiras sociais.* Ed. Maria de Lourdes Saraiva. Lisboa: Europa-América, 1975. 263 pp.
    Auto da Índia (pp. 27-52); *Quem tem farelos?* (pp. 53-81); *Inês Pereira* (pp. 82-132); *O Juiz da Beira* (pp. 133-72); *Farsa dos almocreves* (pp. 173-208); *Romagem dos agravados* (pp. 209-63).

33 See below, no. 456.

ii. Poetry

34 *Poesías.* Ed. Dámaso Alonso. México: Séneca, 1940. 85 pp. The Spanish lyrics of Gil Vicente. Originally published in *Cruz y Raya*, 10 (1934), 115-56.

Reviews:
.1. J. Mañach, *RHM*, II (1936), 108-9.
.2. J. Herrera Petere, 'Oportunidad de Gil Vicente,' *Taller*, II (1940), 53-4.
.3. L.B. Simpson, *Hispania*, XXIII (1940), 300.

35 *A poesia religiosa na literatura portuguesa.* Ed. Augusto César Pires de Lima. Porto: Domingos Barreira, 1942, pp. 53-5.
Three lyrics by Gil Vicente.

36 *Antologia de poesias religiosas desde o século XV, que abre com a Oração do Justo Juiz, de el-Rei D. Duarte, até aos nossos tempos, incluindo romances e cantigas da tradição popular.* Ed. Guilherme Leite de Faria. Lisboa: Edições Gama, 1947, pp. 38-48.
Five lyrics.

37 *The Oxford Book of Portuguese Verse: XIIth Century-XXth Century.* Ed. Aubrey F.G. Bell. 2nd ed. by B. Vidigal. Oxford: Clarendon Press, 1952, pp. 88-92.
Ten lyrics.
Review:
.1. Anon., *TLS* (2 January 1953), p. 6.

38 *Poesías de Gil Vicente.* Ed. Vicente Rojo. México: Librería Madero, 1957. 44 pp.
Thirty Spanish poems.

39 *Líricas portuguesas (1ª série).* Ed. José Régio. 3rd rev. & expanded ed. Lisboa: Portugália, 1959.
Five lyrics.

40 *The Penguin Book of Spanish Verse.* Ed. J.M. Cohen. Rev. ed. Harmondsworth: Penguin Books, 1960.
Six lyrics accompanied by prose translations.

41 *Las mil mejores poesías de la lengua castellana (ocho siglos de poesía española e hispanoamericana).* Ed. José Bergua. 20th ed. Madrid: Ediciones Ibéricas, 1962.
Two lyrics.

41A *The Heath Anthology of Spanish Poetry: with an Introductory Essay on the Development of Metrical Forms.* Ed. Janet H. Perry. Boston: D.C. Heath, 1953, pp. 187-8. Published simultaneously as *The Harrap Anthology . . .* London: George G. Harrap.
Four lyrics.

42 Sainz de Robles, Federico Carlos. *Historia y antología de la poesía española (en lengua castellana) del siglo X al XX.* 4th rev. & expanded ed. Madrid: Aguilar, 1964, pp. 525-8.
Thirteen lyrics.

43   *An Anthology of Spanish Poetry (1500-1700).* Part I: *1500-1580.* Ed.
      Arthur Terry. Oxford: Pergamon Press, 1965.
      Six lyrics.

44   *Líricas de Gil Vicente.* Ed. João de Almeida Lucas. 2nd ed. Lisboa: A.M.
      Teixeira, 1965. 110 pp. (First ed., 1943)

45   Lopes-Graça, F. 'Tres líricas espirituais de Gil Vicente para quarteto vocal
      masculino.' *Vértice*, XXV (1965), [831-40]
      Musical scores: 1. "Chacota de Natal" (*Auto pastoril português*). 2. "Vilan-
      cete pastoril" (*Auto da história de Deus*). 3. "Canto dos cavaleiros de
      Cristo" (*Auto da Barca do Inferno*).

46   *The Oxford Book of Spanish Verse: XIIIth Century-XXth Century.*
      Ed. James Fitzmaurice-Kelly. 2nd ed. by J.B. Trend. Oxford: Clarendon
      Press, 1965.
      Six lyrics.

47   *Poesía.* Ed. Thomas R. Hart. Salamanca: Anaya, 1965. 68 pp.
      Thirty-five lyrics in Spanish—including the "Sermão"—and twenty-five in
      Portuguese.
      Review:
      .1. Leif Sletsjǿe, *StN*, XXXVIII (1966), 136-9.

48   *Antología general de la literatura española (prosa y verso).* Ed. Juan
      Chabas. La Habana: Editora Pedagógica, 1966.
      Six lyrics.

49   *Lírica hispánica de tipo popular: Edad Media y Renacimiento.* Ed. Margit
      Frenk Alatorre. México: Universidad Nacional Autónoma, 1966. xxix +
      271 pp.
      Thirty-nine lyrics.
      Reviews:
      .1. Erika Lorenz, *RJ*, (1968), 345-7.
      .2. Leonardo Romero Tobar, *RdL*, XXXIII (1968), 177.
      .3. C.C. Smith, *BHS*, XLVI (1969), 86.

50   *Pequeno guia da poesia portuguêsa.* Ed. Theodemiro Tostes. Pôrto Alegre:
      Globo, 1967. 88 pp.
      Three lyrics.

51   *A Critical Anthology of Spanish Verse.* Ed. E. Allison Peers. New York:
      Greenwood Press, 1968.
      Reprint of the 1949 edition (Berkeley: University of California Press).
      Two lyrics.

52   *Antología de la poesía española: lírica de tipo tradicional.* Ed. Dámaso
      Alonso & José Manuel Blecua. 2nd rev. ed. Madrid: Gredos, 1969. lxxxvi +
      265 pp. 1st ed. 1956.

Includes twelve of Gil Vicente's poems, reprinted from Alonso's edition—see no. 34 above.

Reviews:
.1. Manuel Alvar, *RFE*, XL (1956), 261.
.2. I.S. Révah, *BEP*, XX (1957), 243.
.3. Margit Frenk Alatorre, *NRFH*, XIII (1959), 360-2.

52A *Antología della letteratura portoghese*. Ed. Cesco Vian. Milano: Fabbri, 1969. 399 pp.

53 *Spanish Poetry from its Beginnings through the Nineteenth Century: An Anthology*. Ed. Willis Barnstone. New York: Oxford University Press, 1970.
Nine lyrics.
Review:
.1. Frank Pierce, *BHS*, L (1973), 166-7.

53A *Diez siglos de poesía castellana*. Ed. Vicente Gaos. Madrid: Alianza Editorial, 1975, pp. 79-82.
Six lyrics.

54* *Poetas quinhentistas: Gil Vicente, Bernardim Ribeiro, Sá de Miranda, Luís de Camões*. Ed. Eduardo Pinheiro. Porto: Figueirinhas, n.d. 102 pp.

55 See also below, nos 376A, 450, 463, 603.

iii. Drama and Poetry

56 *Obras en español*. Ed. Ricardo E. Molinari. Buenos Aires: Nuevo Romance, 1942. 265 pp.
Auto pastoril castelhano, Auto dos Reis Magos, Auto da sibila Cassandra, Auto dos Quatro Tempos, Auto da Barca da Glória, Auto de S. Martinho, Comédia do viúvo, Dom Duardos, "Versos líricos y fragmentos" (pp. 251-61).

57 *Obra teatral y poética*. Ed. Alonso Zamora Vicente. Monterrey, Mexico: Ediciones Oasis, 1963. 125 pp.
Comedia del viudo (pp. 22-78); *Auto pastoril castellano* (pp. 80-111); "Fragmentos de poesías y canciones" (pp. 115-23).

58 *Teatro y poesía*. Ed. Concha de Salamanca. 2nd ed. Madrid: Aguilar, 1963. 481 pp.
First ed., 1946. *Monólogo del vaquerizo, Auto pastoril castellano, Auto de los Reyes Magos, Auto de la sibila Casandra, Auto de las Cuatro Estaciones, La Barca de la Gloria, Auto de San Martín, Comedia del viudo, Amadis de Gaula, Farsa de las gitanas*; "Poesías y fragmentos" (pp. 391-465): thirty-one Spanish lyrics, plus the "Sermón" and the "Trovas a Felipe Guillén".

59 *Antología general de la literatura española*. I: *Desde los orígenes hasta 1700*. Ed. Ángel del Río & Amelia A. de del Río. Revised ed. New York:

Holt, Rinehart &Winston, 1966, pp. 241-51.
Selections; includes an almost complete text of the *Auto da sibila Cassandra.*

60 *Don Duardos, autos y selección poética.* Ed. Mercedes Guillén. Madrid:
Taurus, 1966. 185 pp.
Includes also: *Auto de la sibila Casandra, Auto de la Barca de la Gloria*,
and twenty-nine Spanish lyrics (pp. 169-84).
Review:
.1. Fernando Ponce, *ELit*, 354 (8 October 1966), 24.

61* *Os grandes escritores do Renascimento. Textos do século XVI.* Ed.
Feliciano Ramos & Luís Amaro de Oliveira. Braga: Livraria Cruz, 1968.
626 pp.

62 *Antología de la literatura española.* I: *siglo XI al XVII.* Ed. Germán
Bleiberg. Madrid: Alianza Editorial, 1969. 507 pp.
Selections from the *Auto da sibila Cassandra* plus one poem (pp. 250-2).

C. Individual Plays

Monólogo do vaqueiro (1502)

63 *Auto da visitação (também chamado Monólogo do vaqueiro), acompanhado da versão portuguesa de Paulo Quintela.* Publica-o o Teatro dos
Estudantes da Universidade de Coimbra para comemorar o 450º ani-
versário do nascimento do teatro português. Coimbra: Atlântida, 1952.
13 pp.

64 *A visitação de Gil Vicente à rainha parida Dona Maria. Ensaios de identificação literária e de encenação.* Ed. Joaquim de Oliveira. Lisboa: A. Pinto,
1953. 48 pp.
Text on pp. 35-43. Also: Lisboa: Revista de Portugual, 1961.
Review:
.1. João de Castro Osório, *Ocidente*, XLV (1953), 191-4.

65 Pestana, Sebastião. 'O *Auto da visitação* de Gil Vicente.' In *Homenaje a
Elías Serra Ráfols.* Vol. III. Tenerife: Universidad de La Laguna, 1970,
pp. 137-70.
Critical edition. Text on pp. 155-8. There is a facsimile reproduction of
the 1562 text after p. 170.

66 See also above, nos 1-5, 16, 58.

Auto de São Martinho (1504)

67 *Auto de São Martinho.* First play in *Autos sacramentales desde su origen
hasta fines del siglo XVII.* Ed. Eduardo González Pedroso. Biblioteca de
Autores Españoles, LVIII. Madrid: Rivadeneyra, 1952. Reprint of first
ed. (1865).

68 See also above, nos 1-5, 16, 56, 58.

Auto da Índia (1509)

69   See above, nos 1-5, 28-9 and below, no. 244.

Auto pastoril castelhano (1509)

70   See above, nos 1-5, 16, 56-8.

Auto dos Reis Magos (1510)

71   See above, nos 1-5, 16, 56, 58.

Auto da Fé (1510)

72*   'Auto da Fé, traducido e acomodado à cena por F. Ventura.' *Mensário de Casas do Povo*, 246 (1966).

73   See also above, nos 1-5.

O velho da horta (1512)

74   *O velho da horta.* Ed. João de Almeida Lucas. Lisboa: Edições Ocidente, 1943. 200 pp.

75   See also above, nos 1-5, 18, 27.

Auto dos Quatro Tempos (1513)

76.   See above, nos 1-5, 16, 56, 58.

Auto da sibila Cassandra (1513)

77   *Representación del auto de la Sibila Casandra.* Cuatro palabras explicativas, por Luis Masriera. Barcelona: Archivo Histórico de la Ciudad, 1941. 55 pp., plus plates and music.

77A   See also above, nos 1-5, 16, 56, 58-60.

Exortação da guerra (1514)

78   *Exortação da guerra.* Ed. Francisco Júlio Martins Sequeira. Lisboa: Francisco Franco, n.d. 84 pp.

79   *Exortação da guerra.* Ed. Augusto César Pires de Lima. Porto: Domingos Barreira, 1943. 93 pp.
      Review (of the 1932 edition):
      .1. F. Krüger, *VKR*, V (1932), 273.

80   *Tragicomédia da Exortação da guerra.* Ed. João de Almeida Lucas. Lisboa: Edições Ocidente, 1944. 174 pp.

81   See also above, nos 1-5, 6, 26.

Quem tem farelos? (1515)

82*   *Quem tem farelos?.* Ed. J. Dias da Silva. In his *Colectânea.* 2nd ed. Porto: Educação Nacional, 1944. 171 pp.

83   *Quem tem farelos?.* Ed. Ernesto de Campos de Andrada. Lisboa: Seara

Nova, 1965. 106 pp.
Reprint of the 1938 edition.

84   See also above, nos 1-5, 6, 13, 27-9.

Auto de Mofina Mendes (1515)

85   See above, nos 1-4, 10, 15, 27, 31.

Auto da Barca do Inferno (1517)

86   *Auto da Barca do Inferno (según la edición de 1517).* Ed. Charles David
     Ley. Madrid: CSIC, 1946. 79 pp.

87   *Auto de moralidade da Embarcação do Inferno. Textos das duas primeiras
     edições avulsas e das Copilações estudados por Paulo Quintela. Com um
     apêndice que contém a "Tragicomedia alegórica del Parayso y del Inferno".*
     Coimbra: Atlântida, 1946. cxv + 341 + 11 pp.
     Reviews:
     .1. A.J. Saraiva, *Mundo Literário*, 50 (1947), 9-10.
     .2. L. Silveira, *Ocidente*, XXXI (1947), 49-50.
     .3. J.-B. Aquarone, *RLR*, LXX (1948), 56-8.
     .4. Eugenio Asensio, *RFE*, XXXVII (1953), 279-86.

88   *Recherches sur les oeuvres de Gil Vicente.* I: *Édition critique du premier
     Auto das Barcas.* Ed. I.S. Révah. Lisbonne: Institut Français au Portugal,
     1951. xi + 185 pp.
     Reviews:
     .1. Marcel Bataillon, *BH*, LIII (1951), 206-12.
     .2. J. do Prado Coelho, *BdF*, XII (1951), 210-13.
     .3. Joseph E. Gillet, *HR*, XX (1952), 337-40.
     .4. Eugenio Asensio, *RFE*, XXXVII (1953), 279-86.
     .5. P. Groult, *LR*, VIII (1954), 280-2.

89   *Auto da Barca do Inferno.* Ed. Paulo Quintela. Lisboa: Artis, 1954. xxxv +
     135 pp.

90   *Auto da moralidade.* Nota introdutória de I.S. Révah. Lisboa: O Mundo do
     Livro, 1959. xx + 18 pp.
     Facsimile reproduction of the 1517 edition.
     Reviews:
     .1. I.S. Révah, *BEP*, XXII (1959-60), 304.
     .2. Gerald Moser, *Hispania*, XLIII (1960), 282-3.

91   *Auto da Barca do Inferno.* Lisboa: Expresso, 1969. [16] pp.
     Facsimile of the 1586 text.

92   *Auto da Barca do Inferno.* Ed. Maria da Conceição Gonçalves. Porto:
     Início, 1970. 78 pp.

93   See also above, nos 1-4, 13-14, 18, 24, 27-8, 32; and below, no. 244.

Auto da Alma (1518)

94   *Auto da Alma.* Ed. Francisco Júlio Martins Sequeira. Lisboa: Francisco Franco [1943?]. 92 pp.

95   *Auto da Alma.* In *Textos quinhentistas.* Ed. Álvaro Ferdinando de Sousa da Silveira. Rio de Janeiro: Imprensa Nacional, 1945, pp. 263-344.
      Review:
      .1. Felisberto Martins, *Brasília*, IV (1949), 504-7.

96   *Auto da Alma.* Ed. António Manarte. Porto: Livraria Simões Lopes [1948]. 47 pp.

97   *Auto da Alma.* Prefácio por Eduardo Antonino Pestana, notas e glossário por Sebastião Pestana. Lisboa: Studium, 1948. 68 pp.

98   *Auto da Alma.* In *Textos anotados de Camões e Gil Vicente: excertos de "Os Lusíadas". "Auto da Alma". Sonetos e canções.* Ed. António Manarte. Porto: Livraria Simões Lopes, 1949. 222 pp.

99   *Auto da Alma.* In *Textos literários de Gil Vicente e Luís de Camões.* Ed. João de Almeida Lucas. Lisboa: Francisco Franco, 1950. 225 pp.

99A   *Auto da Alma.* In Gonçalves Neto, Bernardo. *Camões e Gil Vicente. Interpretação e comentário.* 4th ed. Santarém: Tip. Dias Ferreira, 1951, pp. 7-38 (text), 61-86 (notes).

100   *Auto da Alma. Texto fac-similado da edição de 1562 e texto fixado por Sebastião Pestana.* Prefácio de Eduardo Antonino Pestana. Anotações, vocabulários, subsídios para o estudo da métrica e dicionário de rimas de Sebastião Pestana. Lisboa: Revista de Portugal, 1951. 329 pp.
      Reviews:
      .1. F. Costa Marques, *Brasília,* VI (1951), 399-400.
      .2. Eva Salomonski. *Vox Romanica*, XII (1951), 198-9.
      .3. A. Veloso, *RdP*, XVI (1951), 306.
      .4. Manuel de Paiva Boléo, *RPF*, V (1952), 370.

101   *Gil Vicente e "Auto da Alma". Estética e encenação.* Ed. Joaquim de Oliveira. Lisboa: Livraria da Trindade, 1952. 144 pp. Text on pp. 49-111.
      Review:
      .1. João de Castro Osório, *Ocidente*, XLII (1952), 264-5.

102   *Auto da Alma.* Ed. Reis Brasil [José Gomes Bras] . Lisboa: Liceu Nacional de Santarém, 1956. 71 pp.
      (Also 1961, 1965)

103   *Auto da Alma.* In *"Auto da Alma" de Gil Vicente e sonetos e canções de Camões.* Ed. Joaquim Simão Portugal & Manuel Francisco Catarino. Porto: Porto Editora, 1958. 175 pp.

104   *Auto da Alma*. Ed. Feliciano Ramos. Braga: Livraria Cruz, 1962. 83 pp.

105   *Auto da Alma*. Ed. Manuel dos Santos Alves. Coimbra: Atlântida, 1964. 96 pp.

106   *Auto da Alma*. Ed. A. Nunes de Almeida. Lisboa: Aviz, 1965. 91 pp.

107   'Gil Vicente. *Auto da Alma*. Adaptação de Walmir Ayala.' *Dionysos*, X, 12 (September 1965), 70-93.

108   *Auto da Alma*. Ed. Augusto César Pires de Lima. 10th ed. Porto: Domingos Barreira, 1967. 86 pp.
(First ed.: Porto: Tip. da Enciclopédia Portuguesa, 1926)
> *Review* (of the 3rd edition, 1940):
> .1. V.A. Ferreira, *Biblos*, XVII (1941), 375-7.

109   *Auto da Alma*. Ed. Maria da Conceição Gonçalves. Porto: Início, 1970. 59 pp.

110   *Auto da Alma*. Edição escolar com introdução, notas, glossário e questionário ideológico, estilístico e gramatical e precedida do texto facsimilado da primeira edição (1562) por Júlio Martins e Jaime da Mota. 5th ed. Lisboa: Livraria Didáctica, 1971. 91 pp.
(Also 1961, 1965, 1967, 1969)

111   *Auto da Alma*. In *"Auto da Alma" de Gil Vicente. Sonetos e canções de Camões (para o 5º ano dos liceus)*. Ed. Maria Helena Meireles. Porto: Edições ASA, n.d., pp. 7-45.

112   See also above, nos 1-4, 6, 10, 13, 26-8, 31.

Auto da Barca do Purgatório (1518)

113   *Auto da Barca do Purgatório*. Ed. Paulo Quintela. Lisboa: Artis, 1955. 99 pp.

114   *Auto da Barca do Purgatório*. Ed. Maria da Conceição Gonçalves. Porto: Início, 1970. 69 pp.

115   See also above, nos 1-4, 14, 24, 31-2.

Auto da Barca da Glória (1519)

116   *Auto da Embarcação da Glória. O texto original segundo a edição de 1562, com versão portuguesa*. Introdução e notas de Paulo Quintela. Coimbra: Coimbra Editora, 1941. lxviii + 100 pp.
> *Review:*
> .1. W. Mulertt, *LGRP*, LXIV (1943), cols 307-9.

117*   *Auto da Barca da Glória com versão portuguesa de Paulo Quintela*. Lisboa: Artis, 1956.

118   See also above, nos 1-4, 14, 16, 24, 32, 56, 58, 60.

Auto da Fama (1520)

119   See above, nos 1-4.

Côrtes de Júpiter (1521)

120   See above, nos 1-4, 6, 29.

Comédia de Rubena (1521)

121   *Comédia de Rubena.* Ed. Giuseppe Tavani. Officina Romanica, III. Studi
       e Testi Portoghesi e Brasiliani, II. Roma: Ateneo, 1965. 167 pp.
       Reviews:
       .1. Aldo Menichetti, *CN*, XXVI (1966), 309.
       .2. Thomas R. Hart, *MLN*, LXXXII (1967), 645-6.
       .3. Donatella Ferro, *Annali della Facoltà di Lingue e Letterature
           Straniere di Ca'Foscari*, VII (1968), 188-90.
       .4. Eugenio Asensio, *NRFH*, XIX (1970), 146-51.

122   See also above, nos 1-4, 15.

Auto das ciganas (1521)

123   See above, nos 1-4, 16, 58.

Tragicomédia de Dom Duardos (1522)

124   *Tragicomedia de Don Duardos. Texto, estudios y notas.* Ed. Dámaso
       Alonso. Madrid: CSIC, 1942. 329 pp. (See also following entry)
       Reviews:
       .1. Amado Alonso, *RFH*, IV (1942), 282-5.
       .2. Rafael Ferreres, *Escorial*, VII (1942), 456-62.
       .3. Marcel Bataillon, *BH*, XLV (1943), 211-14.
       .4. A.J. da Costa Pimpão, *Biblos*, XIX (1943), 583-5.
       .5. W.J. Entwistle, *MLR*, XXXVIII (1943), 163-5.
       .6. M. García Blanco, *Revista de la Universidad de Madrid*, 1 (1943),
           265-70.
       .7. M. Romera-Navarro, *HR*, XI (1943), 355-9.
       .8. W., *ZRP*, LXIII (1943), 434-6.

125   *Tragicomedia de Don Duardos.* Ed. Dámaso Alonso. Madrid: CSIC, 1942.
       109 pp.
       The text of the above with a short introduction and no notes.

126   *Tragicomedia de Don Duardos.* Ed. Giovanni Maria Bertini. Torino:
       Chiantore, 1945. 127 pp.

127   *Tragicomedia de Don Duardos.* In *El teatro anterior a Lope de Vega.* Ed.
       Everett W. Hesse & Juan O. Valencià. Madrid: Alcalá, 1971, pp. 119-98.
       The text is based on Dámaso Alonso's edition.

128   See also above, nos 1-4, 16, 56, 60; and below, nos 172, 456.

Auto de Inês Pereira (1523)

129   *Actividade dramática de Gil Vicente e "Farsa de Inês Pereira".* Ed. M. Marques Braga. Lisboa: Cosmos, 1941. 127 pp.
      Review:
      .1. Paulo Quintela, *Biblos*, XVII (1941), 786-90.

130   *Farsa de Inês Pereira.* Ed. Francisco Torrinha & Augusto César Pires de Lima. Porto: Domingos Barreira, 1941. 91 pp.
      Review (of the 1932 edition):
      .1. F. Krüger, *VKR*, V (1932), 273.

131*   *Encenação da "Farsa de Inez Pereira" de Gil Vicente.* Ed. Joaquim de Oliveira. Lisboa: Revista "De Teatro", 194-. 59 pp.

132   *Auto de Inês Pereira.* Ed. Paulo Quintela. Lisboa: Artis, 1953. xxvi + 115 pp.

133   *Recherches sur les oeuvres de Gil Vicente.* II: *Édition critique de l' "Auto de Inês Pereira".* Ed. I.S. Révah. Lisbonne: Institut Français au Portugal, 1955. 276 pp.
      First appeared in *BHTP*, III (1952), 196-265; IV (1953), 75-119, 239-90; V (1954), 227-323.
      Review:
      .1. A.E. Sloman, *BHS*, XXXIV (1957), 236-7.

134   Saviotti, Gino. *'Inês Pereira.* Ópera cómica em 3 actos inspirada nas farsas de Gil Vicente.' *EIP*, XXVIII (1967), 119-74.

135   *A farsa de Inês Pereira.* Ed. Maria da Conceição Gonçalves. Porto: Início, 1970. 64 pp.

136   *Farsa de Inês Pereira.* Ed. Manuel dos Santos Alves. Lisboa: Emp. Literária Fluminense, 1974. 87 pp.

137   *Farsa de Inês Pereira.* Ed. Albano Monteiro Soares. Porto: Porto Editora, 1975. 95 pp.

138   See also above, nos 1-4, 6, 8, 13, 18, 27-8, 31.

Auto pastoril português (1523)

139   *'Auto pastoril português.* Adaptação de Armando Tavares de Medeiros.' *Insulana*, XX (1966), 98-127.

140   See also above, nos 1-4.

Tragicomédia de Amadis de Gaula (1523)

141   *Tragicomedia de Amadís de Gaula.* Ed. T.P. Waldron. Manchester: Manchester University Press, 1959. 111 pp.
      Originally his M.A. thesis for King's College, London, 1953.
      Reviews:
      .1. I.S. Révah, *BEP*, XXII (1959-60), 308.

.2. B.W. Ellis, *JAULLA*, 13 (1960), 104-5.
.3. Stephen Reckert, *BHS*, XXXVII (1960), 251-2.
.4. C.A. Jones, *HR*, XXIX (1961), 147-8.
.5. John Lihani, *MLN*, LXXVI (1961), 284-6.
.6. Jack H. Parker, *Hispania*, XLIV (1961), 197-8.

142 See also above, nos 1-4, 16, 58.

Comédia do viúvo (1524)

143 Titterington, Ann. "A Critical Edition of Gil Vicente's *Comédia do viúvo*, with Introduction and Philological Notes." M.A. thesis, Queen Mary College, London, 1962. 158 pp.

144 *Comedia del viudo*. Ed. Alonso Zamora Vicente. Publicaçaões do Centro de Estudos Filológicos, XIII. Lisboa: Instituto de Alta Cultura, 1962. 98 pp.
   Reviews:
   .1. A.B., *Brotéria*, LXXV (1962), 246.
   .2. M.J. Moura Santos, *RPF*, XII (1962-3), 769-70.
   .3. Anon., *Índice Cultural Español*, XVII (1963), 115.
   .4. M. de Jong, *Neophilologus*, XLVII (1963), 157-8.
   .5. Henri Guiter, *RLR*, LXXV (1963), 290-1.
   .6. Z. Hampejs, *PP*, VI (1963), 442-3.
   .7. Raymond Sayers, *RHM*, XXIX (1963), 76.
   .8. Charlotte Stern, *HR*, XXXI (1963), 359-62.
   .9. M. Molho, *BH*, LXVI (1964), 225-7.
   .10. Giuseppe Tavani, *RJ*, XVI (1965), 385-7.

145 See also above, nos 1-5, 16, 56-8.

Frágua de Amor (1524)

146 See above, nos 1-4, 29.

Farsa dos físicos (1524)
147 *Auto chamado Farsa dos físicos*. Ed. Alberto da Rocha Brito. Lisboa: Laboratórios de Bemfica, 1946. 141 pp.

148 See also above, nos 1-4.

O Juiz da Beira (1525 or 1526)

149 See above, nos 1-4.

Templo de Apolo (1526)

150 See above, nos 1-4.

Auto da feira (1526)

151 See above, nos 1-4, 13, 27-8, 31; and below, no. 244.

Nau de amores (1527)

152 See above, nos 1-4.

Comédia sobre a divisa da cidade de Coimbra (1527)

153   Rangel-Guerrero, Daniel. "Gil Vicente. *Comédia sobre a divisa da cidade de Coimbra*, con una introducción y notas." Dissertation, University of Oregon, 1967. 136 pp.
See *DA*, XXVIII(1967-8), 2219A-2220A.

154   See also above, nos 1-4.

Farsa dos almocreves (1527)

155   See above, nos 1-4, 26-7.

Tragicomédia pastoril da Serra da Estrêla (1527)

156   *Tragicomédia pastoril da Serra da Estrêla. Texto princeps. Texto modernizado.* Ed. Álvaro Júlio da Costa Pimpão. Revised ed. Coimbra: Atlântida, 1963. 138 pp.
    Review (of the 1941 edition):
    .1. Werner Mulertt, *LGRP*, LXIII (1942), col. 328.

157   See also above, nos 1-4, 26.

Breve sumário da história de Deus (1527)

158   *Breve sumário da história de Deus.* Ed. João de Almeida Lucas. Lisboa: A.M. Teixeira, 1943. 102 pp.

159   See also above, nos 1-4, 28.

Diálogo sobre a ressurreição de Cristo (1527)

160   See above, nos 1-4.

Auto das fadas (1527)

161   See above, nos 1-5.

Auto da festa (1527 or 1528)

162   See above, nos 1-4.

O triunfo do Inverno (1529)

163   See above, nos 1-4, 29.

O clérigo da Beira (1529 or 1530)

164   See above, nos 1-4.

Auto da Lusitânia (1532)

165   See above, nos 1-4, 27, 30-1.

Romagem de agravados (1533)

166   *Romagem d'agravados.* Ed. Paul Teyssier. Paris: Éditions Hispaniques, 1975. 147 pp.

167   See also above, nos 1-4, 27.

Auto da Cananeia (1534)

168   See above, nos 1-4.

Floresta de enganos (1536)

169   *A Critical Edition with Introduction and Notes of Gil Vicente's "Floresta de enganos"*. Ed. Constantine C. Stathatos. University of North Carolina Studies in the Romance Languages and Literatures, CXXV. Chapel Hill: University of North Carolina Press, 1972. 138 pp.
       Originally his dissertation for the University of Oregon, 1970. See *DAI*, XXXI (1970-1), 3521A.
       Review:
       .1. Alice R. Clemente, *MLN*, LXXXIX (1974), 323-5.

170   See also above, nos 1-4.

D. Miscellaneous Works

171   Michaëlis de Vasconcelos, Carolina. *Notas vicentinas: preliminares duma edição crítica das obras de Gil Vicente (Notas I a V)*. 2nd ed. Lisboa: Revista "Ocidente", 1949. 661 pp.
       Includes the text of the "Romance à morte del Rei Dom Manuel e à aclamação de Dom João terceiro" of a *fôlha volante* and gives the 1562 variants (pp. 128-32).

172   Révah, I.S. "Édition critique du *romance* de Don Duardos et Flérida." *BHTP*, III (1952), 107-39.
       Révah establishes a critical text from the several versions of this ballad.

173   *Il Pranto de Maria Parda*. Ed. Luciana Stegagno Picchio. Napoli: Istituto Universitario Orientale, 1963. 127 pp.
       Edition of the Harvard University copy. Appeared first in *AION-SR*, V (1963), 35-126.
       Reviews:
       .1. C. Cordié, *Paideia*, XIX (1964), 418.
       .2. I.S. Révah, *BEP*, XXV (1964), 273-7.

174   *O "Pranto de Maria Parda" de Gil Vicente*. Ed. Sebastião Pestana. Sá da Bandeira, Angola: Gráfica Huíla, 1975. 394 pp.
       Facsimile reproduction of the 1522 *pliego suelto* text on pp. 93-102. Pestana's text on 103-18. In addition to a long introduction, notes, variants, metrical analysis, vocabulary, etc., there are facsimiles of the texts of 1562, 1586, 1643, 1665.

175   See also above, nos 1-5, 8, 28, 47, 58.

TRANSLATIONS

A. Drama

English

176* *Cassandra the Sibyl.* Trans. Rachel Benson. In *Early Spanish Plays*. Ed. Robert O'Brien. New York: Las Américas, 1964. Vol. I.

177 *Don Duardos.* Trans. Mary Borelli. Columbia, South Carolina, 1976. vi + 45 pp.

178 *Four Plays.* Ed. & trans. Aubrey F.G. Bell. See above, no. 26.

179 *Four Plays*. Trans. Jill Booty. *Tulane Drama Review*, V (1961), 160-86. Reprinted in *Early Spanish Plays*, ed. Robert O'Brien (New York: Las Américas, 1964), vol. II.
Prose translations of *The Three Wise Men (Auto dos Reis Magos); The Serenade (Quem tem farelos?); The Sailor's Wife (Auto da Índia); The Widower's Comedy (Comédia do viúvo).*

180 *The Ship of Hell.* Trans. A.F. Gerald [A.F.G. Bell]. Lisboa: Agência Geral do Ultramar, 1954. 35 pp.
Verse translation of the *Barca do Inferno* reprinted from *The Ship of Hell*, trans. A.F. Gerald (Watford: Voss & Michael, 1929).
Review:
.1. M. Almeida, *Brotéria*, LX (1955), 579-80.

181 *The Ship of Hell (A Trilogy).* Trans. Aubrey F.G. Bell. In *Early Spanish Plays*. Ed. Robert O'Brien. New York: Las Américas, 1964. Vol. I. Reprint of *The Ship of Hell* (Watford: Voss & Michael, 1929). Includes verse translations of the *Barca do Inferno*, the *Barca do Purgatório* and the *Barca da Glória.*

French

182 *La Barque d'Enfer (1518).* Trans. Claude-Henri Frèches. Paris: Institut Français au Portugal, 1955. 38 pp.

183 *Les Indes (Auto da Índia).* Trans. Claude-Henri Frèches. Lisboa: Livraria Bertrand, 1956. 23 pp.
First appeared in *BEP*, XIX (1955-6), 139-57 ('Avant-propos,' pp. 139-44).

184 *Trilogie des Barques.* Trans. Andrée Crabbé Rocha. Coimbra: Atlântida, 1958. xi + 85 pp.

Galician

185   *A Barca do Inferno.* Trans. Xosé Landeira Yrago. Vigo: Edicions Castrelos, 1970. 46 pp.

German

186   *Geistliche Spiele (Jedermann und Niemand. Das Spiel von den Barken. Das Spiel von der Seele).* Trans. Margarete Kühne. Coimbra: Coimbra Editora, 1940. viii + 182 pp.
       The translation of the *Auto da Alma* appeared first in the *Boletim do Instituto Alemão,* V (1935), 56-82. See also following entry.
       Review:
       .1. Werner Mulertt, *VKR*, XIV (1941), 333-4.

187   *Inês Pereira, eine Posse.* Trans. Moriz Rapp. *Das Spiel von der Seele.* Trans. Margarete Kühne. Coimbra: Atlântida, 1952. 49 pp.

Italian

188   *La sibilla Cassandra.* Trans. Carlo Bo. In *Teatro spagnolo. Raccolta di drammi e commedie dalle origini ai nostri giorni.* Ed. Elio Vittorini. Milano: Bompiani, 1944, pp. 80-90.
       Prose translation.

189   *Teatro.* Trans. Enzio di Poppa Vòlture. 2 vols. Firenze: Sansoni, 1957. Verse translation of Gil Vicente's complete theater. First published in two vols, 1953-4, xlv + 681, 784 pp.
       Reviews:
       .1. Anon., *EIP*, XIII (1954), 96-7.
       .2. Piero Raimondi, *Convivium*, XXIII (1955), 366-7.
       .3. Giuseppe Carlo Rossi, *L'Italia che Scrive*, XXXVIII (1955), 67.

190   *Teatro portoghese e brasiliano.* Ed. & trans. Giuseppe Carlo Rossi. Milano: Nuova Accademia, 1956. 403 pp. + 8 plates.
       Prose translations: *Auto della visitazione (Monologo del vaccaro),* pp. 29-35. *Auto pastorale castigliano*, pp. 37-49. *Auto dell'India*, pp. 51-66. *Auto della Barca dell'Inferno* (of the 1518 ed.), pp. 67-92. *Farsa di Inês Pereira*, pp. 93-119.
       Reviews:
       .1. I.S. Révah, *BEP*, XIX (1955-6), 219.
       .2. A. Carballo Picazo, *RdL*, IX (1956), 173-5.
       .3. Luciana Stegagno Picchio, *Filologia Romanza*, III (1956), 325-35.
       .4. R. Barchiesi, *EIP*, XVI (1957), 65-9.
       .5. Marco Boni. *Nuova Antologia*, XCII (1957), 133-7.
       .6. Hernâni Cidade, *RFLUL*, XXII (1957), 206-8.
       .7. Z. Hampejs, *PP*, I (1958), 128.
       .8. Gerald Moser, *BAbr*, XXXII (1958), 439.

191　*Trilogia delle Barche.* Trans. Gianfranco Contini. In *Teatro religioso del Medioevo fuori d'Italia. Raccolta di testi dal secolo VII al secolo XV.* Ed. Gianfranco Contini. Milano: Bompiani, 1949, pp. 323-72.
Prose translations: *Barca dell'Inferno*, pp. 331-45. *Barca del Purgatorio*, pp. 347-59. *Barca del Paradiso*, pp. 361-72.
　Reviews:
　.1. Anon., *Convivium* (1950), 468-9.
　.2. C.C., *Letterature Moderne*, I (1950), 133-4.

Norwegian

192　Sletsjøe, Leif. *Gil Vicente: Portugisisk dramatiker på grensen mellom Middelalder og Renessance. Med oversettelse av fem av hans spill:* "Gamlingen i haven," "Spillet om sjelen," "Farsen om Inês Pereira," "Kort beretning om Guds historie," "Spillet om Mofina Mendes" [Gil Vicente: Portuguese Dramatist on the Border between the Middle Ages and the Renaissance. With a Translation of Five of his Plays: *O velho da horta* (pp. 81-105), *Auto da Alma* (pp. 106-31), *Farsa de Inês Pereira* (pp. 132-68), *Breve sumário da história de Deus* (pp. 169-201), *Auto da Mofina Mendes* (pp. 202-27)]. Teaterhistorisk Selskap-Skrifter VIII. Oslo: Gyldendal, 1973. 229 pp.
Verse translation.

Portuguese

193　'*A Barca da Glória*. Versão portuguesa de Paulo Quintela.' *Biblos*, XVII (1941), 37-84.
See no. 195 below.

194　*Auto da Barca da Glória.* In *Os autos das Barcas.* Fixação do texto, introdução, notas e tradução do terceiro auto de Luiz Francisco Rebello. 2nd ed. Lisboa: Europa-América, 1975, pp. 121-45.
Verse translation.

195　*Auto da Embarcação da Glória. O texto original segundo a edição de 1562, com versão portuguesa.* Introdução e notas de Paulo Quintela. Coimbra: Coimbra Editora, 1941. lxviii + 100 pp.
Verse translation.
　Review:
　.1. Werner Mulertt, *LGRP*, LXIV (1943), cols 307-9.

196　*Auto da visitação (também chamado "Monólogo do vaqueiro"),* acompanhado da versão portuguesa de Paulo Quintela. Coimbra: Atlântida, 1952. 13 pp.　　Verse translation.

B　*Poetry*

English

197　*An Anthology of Spanish Literature in English Translation.* Ed. Seymour

Resnick &Jeanne Pasmantier. New York: Ungar, 1958. Vol. I.
Includes verse translations of two lyrics from *Cassandra*: "Muy graciosa es la doncella" by Alice Jane McVan (p. 105), and "Dicen que me case yo" by George Ticknor (pp. 105-6).

198 Bowra, C.M. "The Songs of Gil Vicente." In his *Inspiration and Poetry*. London: Macmillan, 1955, pp. 90-111.
Includes his verse translations of: "Branca estais e colorada" (*Feira*), p. 94. "Este é maio, o maio é este" (*Lusitânia*), p. 97. "Qual de nos vem mais cansada" (*Fadas*), p. 99. "A serra é alta, fria e nevosa" (*Almocreves*), p. 101. "Adorae montanhas / o Deos das alturas" (*História de Deus*), p. 102. "Muy graciosa es la doncella" (*Cassandra*), pp. 105-6. "¡A la guerra, / caballeros esforzados!" (*Cassandra*), pp. 107-8. "Tirae os olhos de mim" (*Auto pastoril português*), p. 109. "Remando vam remadores" (*Purgatório*), p. 110. It also includes A.F.G. Bell's verse rendering of "Halcón que se atreve" (*Rubena*), p. 95.

199 Brenan, Gerald. *The Literature of the Spanish People: From Roman Times to the Present Day*. 2nd ed. Cambridge: Cambridge University Press, 1953.
Includes the author's prose translation of "Muy graciosa es la doncella" (*Cassandra*), p. 143.

200 Campbell, Roy. *Collected Poems*. III: *Translations*. Foreword by Edith Sitwell. Chicago: Henry Regnery, 1960.
Verse translations of "Todo o Mundo e Ninguém" (*Lusitânia*), pp. 121-3, and "Remando vam remadores" (*Purgatório*), p. 124.

201 Campbell, Roy. *Selected Poetry*. Ed. J.M. Lalley. Chicago: Henry Regnery, 1968.
Includes the second item of above entry, pp. 207-8.

202 "En la huerta nace la rosa." Trans. Willis Barnstone. *Antioch Review*, XXIV (1964), 90.
From *Quatro Tempos*; verse translation.

203 *Highlights of Spanish Literature: A Bilingual Anthology*. Ed. Seymour Resnick & Jeanne Pasmantier. New York: Ungar, 1963.
Includes the same items as no. 197 above: pp. 113 and 115 respectively.

204 *Hispanic Anthology: Poems Translated from the Spanish by English and North American Poets*. Ed. Thomas Walsh. New York: Kraus Reprint Co., 1969.
Reprint of the 1920 ed. (New York & London: G.P. Putnam's Sons). Includes verse translations of: "Muy graciosa es la doncella" (*Cassandra*) by Thomas Walsh (pp. 163-4). "En la huerta nasce la rosa" (*Quatro Tempos*) by John Bowring (pp. 164-5). "Si dormís, doncella" (*Farelos*) by H.W. Longfellow (p. 165).

205 *A Little Treasury of World Poetry: Translations from the Great Poets of Other Languages (2600 B.C. to 1950 A.D.).* Ed. Hubert Creekmore. New York: Charles Scribner's Sons, 1952.
Verse translations of "Muy graciosa es la doncella" (*Cassandra*) by Alice Jane McVan (pp. 680-1), and of "Si dormís, doncella" (*Farelos*) by H.W. Longfellow (p. 681).

206 Livermore, Ann. 'Gil Vicente and Shakespeare.' *Book Handbook*, II (1951), 1-12.
Includes the author's verse translation of "Por más que la vida pene" (*Inverno*), p. 6.

207 *Lyrics of the Middle Ages*. Ed. Hubert Creekmore. New York: Greenwood Press, 1969.
Seth G. Thornton's verse translations of "Tirai os olhos de mim" (*Auto pastoril português*) and "A suidade na molher / mata o coração e alma" (*Inverno*), p. 111.

208 *Medieval Lyrics of Europe*. Ed. & trans. Willard R. Trask. New York & Cleveland: World, 1969.
Prose translation of "Muy graciosa es la doncella" (*Cassandra*), p. 142.

209 *One Thousand and One Poems of Mankind: Memorable Short Poems from the World's Chief Literatures*. Ed. Henry H. Wells. Atlanta: Tupper and Love, 1953.
John Bowring's verse translation of "Del rosal vengo, mi madre" (*Inverno*), p. 330.

210 *The Penguin Book of Spanish Verse*. Ed. J.M. Cohen. Rev. ed. Harmondsworth: Penguin Books, 1960.
The editor's prose translations of "Dicen que me case yo", " ¡Sañosa está la niña!", "Muy graciosa es la doncella" and " ¡A la guerra, / caballeros esforzados!" (*Cassandra*); "En la huerta nasce la rosa" (*Quatro Tempos*); "Del rosal vengo, mi madre" (*Inverno*): pp. 100-4.

211 "Remando vam remadores." Trans. William Myron Davis. *Southern Review*, II (1966), 126-7.
From *Purgatório*; verse translation (p. 127).

212 *Renaissance and Baroque Lyrics: An Anthology of Translations from the Italian, French and Spanish*. Ed. Harold Martin Priest. Evanston, Illinois: Northwestern University Press, 1962.
Verse translations: Alice Jane McVan, "Muy graciosa es la doncella" (*Cassandra*), p. 185; H.W. Longfellow, "Si dormís, doncella" (*Farelos*), p. 185; Beatrice Gilman Proske, "En el mes era de abril" (*Dom Duardos*), pp. 185-7.

213 *Selections from Spanish Poetry*. Ed. Seymour Resnick. Irvington-on-

Hudson, New York: Harvey House, 1962.
Verse translations from *Cassandra*: Resnick's of "Dicen que me case yo", p. 38. Alice Jane McVan's "Muy graciosa es la doncella", p. 40.

214   *The Singing and the Gold: Poems Translated from World Literature.* Ed. Elinor Parker. New York: Thomas Y. Crowell, 1962.
Same items as no. 205 above: pp. 41 and 148 respectively.

215   *Ten Centuries of Spanish Poetry. An Anthology in English Verse with Original Texts: From the XIth Century to the Generation of 1898.* Ed. Eleanor L. Turnbull. With Introductions by Pedro Salinas. Baltimore: The Johns Hopkins Press, 1955.
Verse translations: Alice Jane McVan's of "Muy graciosa es la doncella" (*Cassandra*), no. 51. Turnbull's "En la huerta nasce la rosa" (*Quatro Tempos*), and "Del rosal vengo, mi madre" (*Inverno*), nos 52 & 53. Aubrey F.G. Bell's "En el mes era de abril" (*Dom Duardos*), no. 54.

216   Ticknor, George. *History of Spanish Literature.* 6th ed., corrected & enlarged. New York: Gordian Press, 1965. Vol. I.
Reprint of the 1891 ed. First ed., New York: Harper & Bros, 1849. Includes the author's verse translations from *Cassandra*: "Dicen que me case yo", p. 301; "¡Sañosa está la niña!", p. 302; "Muy graciosa es la doncella", p. 303,; "¡A la guerra, / caballeros esforzados!", p. 303.

217   *Translation (London).* Ed. Neville Braybrooke & Elizabeth King. London: Phoenix Press, 1945.
No pagination. Includes E. Allison Peers' verse translation of "Muy graciosa es la doncella" (*Cassandra*).

218   *Translations/Comment in Motion*, VII (1969), 211-16.
Verse translations by Grover I. Jacoby: "Dicen que me case yo" (*Cassandra*), p. 211; "En la huerta nasce la rosa" (*Quatro Tempos*), p. 212; "Muy graciosa es la doncella" (*Cassandra*), p. 213; "¡Sañosa está la niña!" (*Cassandra*), p. 214; "Del rosal vengo, mi madre" (*Inverno*), p. 215; "¡A la guerra / caballeros esforzados!" (*Cassandra*), p. 216.

218A   Trend, J.B. No. 469, below, includes a verse translation of "Muy graciosa es la doncella" (*Cassandra*), pp. 163-4.

219   *The World's Best Poems.* Ed. Mark Van Doren & Garibaldi M. Lapolla. Cleveland and New York: World, 1946.
Includes H.W. Longfellow's verse translation of "Si dormís, doncella" (*Farelos*), p. 250.

Italian

220   "Il Trionfo dell'Inverno." Trans. Guido Battelli. *Ocidente*, LXIX (1965), 27-8.
Verse translation. Appeared first in *Portucale*, IX (1936), 200-2.

221 *Orfeo: il tesoro della lirica universale interpretato in versi italiani.* Ed.
Vincenzo Errante &Emilio Mariano. Firenze: Sansoni, 1950.
Includes Piero Raimondi's verse translations of "Los amores de la niña"
(*Lusitânia*), p. 374; "¿Por dó pasaré la sierra?" (*Inverno*), p. 375; "Muy
graciosa es la doncella" (*Cassandra*), p. 375.

222 *Pagine della letteratura portoghese.* Ed. Pasquale Aniel Jannini. Milano:
Nuova Accademia, 1955.
Includes the editor's verse translations of "Oração para Santo Agostinho"
(*Alma*), pp. 70-4; "Falas de amor" (*Velho da horta*), pp. 74-9.

Portuguese

223 *Líricas castelhanas de Gil Vicente em versão portuguesa de Paulo
Quintela.* Coimbra: Atlântida, 1966. xxii + 135 pp.
Verse translations of 57 lyrics and of some fragments from Gil Vicente's
plays. First appeared in *Vértice*, XXV (1965), 733-94.

224 Osório, João de Castro. 'Os poetas do primeiro livro do Florilégio—XI:
Gil Vicente.' In his *Florilégio das poesias portuguesas escritas em castelhano e restituídas à língua nacional.* Lisboa: Império, 1942, pp. 122-36.
Reprinted from *Ocidente*, XV (1941), 321-36. Contains verse renderings
into modern Portuguese of eighteen lyrics (pp. 126-36).

Spanish

225 'Canciones portuguesas de Gil Vicente.' Trans. Dámaso Alonso. In his
Obras completas. II: *Estudios y ensayos sobre literatura. Primera parte:
Desde los orígenes románicos hasta finales del siglo XVI.* Madrid: Gredos,
1973, pp. 465-8.
Verse translations: "Remando vam remadores" (*Purgatório*), pp. 465-6;
"Canas do amor, canas" (*Inês Pereira*), "A serra é alta, fria e nevosa"
(*Almocreves*), p. 466; "Branca estais, colorada" (*Feira*), pp. 466-7;
"A mi seguem os dous açôres" (*Serra da Estrêla*), p. 467; "Quem é a
desposada?" and "Tirai os olhos de mim" (*Auto pastoril português*),
pp. 467-8; "Não me firais, madre" (*Estrêla*), p. 468. First appeared in
Isla, 20 (1940); they were later reprinted in Alonso's *De los siglos
oscuros al de oro* (Madrid: Gredos, 1958), pp. 153-7.

CRITICAL STUDIES

A. Books, monographs, theses, and pamphlets

Note: 'Dissertations' are doctoral dissertations unless otherwise stated. 'Pamphlets' include articles from journals separately published in pamphlet form.

226　Aguiar, Fernando de. *Gil Vicente*. Guimarães: Tip. Minerva, 1968. 104 pp. (From the journal *Gil Vicente)*

227　Almeida, A. Pinto. *Gil Vicente na tradição popular?*. Porto: Domingos Barreira, 1943. 8 pp.

228　Amaral, Alexandre do. *Três nótulas vicentinas:* I. *"Alexander de Aliis."* II. *"Bernardus de Virgo Assumptionis."* III. *"Amor vincit omnia."* Coimbra: Coimbra Editora, 1953. 20 pp.

229　Andrade, M.C. "El religioso disoluto del Renacimiento visto por Gil Vicente." M.A. thesis, Louisiana State University, Baton Rouge, 1968. iv + 79 pp.

230　Andrews, James Richard. "The Artistry of the Plays of Gil Vicente." Dissertation, Princeton University, 1953. 223 pp.
See *DA*, XIV (1954), 116-17.

231*　Azevedo, Narciso de. *Origens do teatro vicentino.* I: *Uma fonte comum do "Auto da Alma" e do "Fausto"*. Porto: Educação Nacional, 1943. 53 pp.

232　Bell, Aubrey F.G. *Estudos vicentinos*. Trans. António Álvaro Dória. Lisboa: Imprensa Nacional, 1940. xvi + 222 pp.
Translation revised by the author. Contains: 'Gil Vicente', pp. 1-40: first published in the *Boletim de Segunda Classe da Academia das Ciências de Lisboa*, IX (1915), 149-83. 'Gil Vicente', pp. 41-112: translation of the introductory essay to *Four Plays of Gil Vicente* (Cambridge: Cambridge University Press, 1920), pp. ix-li. 'Gil Vicente', pp. 113-46: translation of *Gil Vicente* (Oxford University Press, 1921), 70 pp. [reviewed by J.P. Wickersham Crawford, *MPhi*, XX (1922-3), 437-9]. 'Gil Vicente', pp. 147-54: translation of entry in the *Encyclopaedia Britannica*, 14th ed. (1929). 'Notas para uma edição de Gil Vicente', pp. 155-86: first appeared in English in *Revue Hispanique*, LXXVII (1929), 382-408. 'Postfácio' (bibliography), pp. 187-201.

233*　Bonito, Porfírio Augusto Rebelo. *A música dos autos de Gil Vicente*.

Porto, 1958.
(From *Revista de Guimarães* and *Gil Vicente*)

234　Braamcamp Freire, Anselmo. *Vida e obras de Gil Vicente "trovador, mestre da Balança".* 2nd rev. ed. Lisboa: Revista Ocidente, 1944. 635 pp. + 19 plates.
From *Ocidente*, V (1939), 5-16, 224-56; VI (1939), 65-80, 225-40, 401-16; VII (1939), 33-48, 225-40, 353-68; VIII (1939-40), 49-64, 385-400, 545-60; IX (1940), 65-80, 193-208, 433-48; X (1940), 49-64, 209-24, 365-80; XI (1940), 49-64, 209-24, 345-60; XII (1941), 37-52, 213-28, 357-72; XIII (1941), 33-48, 225-40, 429-44; XIV (1941), 49-64, 225-40, 361-76; XV (1941), 65-80, 177-92, 369-85; XXII (1944), 5-8. The *Ocidente* articles are a reworking of the original version published in *RdH*, VI (1917), 1-46, 121-88, 289-346; VII (1918), 1-46, 109-48. Contains: 'Preâmbulo,' pp. 13-20. 'Dados biográficos (Identificação do poeta e do ourives; Primórdios indecisos—1460 (?)-1502; No reinado de D. Manuel—1502-1521; Na côrte de D. João III—1521-1536),' pp. 21-324. 'Os filhos de Gil Vicente,' pp. 325-53. 'Tentativa bibliográfica,' pp. 354-98. 'Censura inquisitorial,' pp. 399-463. 'Confrontação de textos vicentinos,' pp. 464-98 (the texts of the Palha copy and of 1562 of the *Pranto de Maria Parda*, pp. 465-73; those of the Madrid copy of the *fôlha volante* and of 1562 of *Inês Pereira*, pp. 473-98). 'Canto, dança e música nos autos de Gil Vicente,' pp. 499-516. 'Documentos—I a XXV,' pp. 517-37. 'Cronologia vicentina,' pp. 539-64. 'Índices,' pp. 565-633. The lengthy index appears only in the book version, which also has illustrations and a new prologue.

235　Branco, Carlos. *O culto da Virgem na obra de Gil Vicente.* Lisboa: Oficina Gráfica Ltda, 1941. 16 pp.
(From *Anuário do Liceu de Gil Vicente*)

236　Brasil, Reis [José Gomes Bras]. *As determinantes do humanismo na obra de Gil Vicente.* Figueira da Foz, 1961. 29 pp.
First published in *Miscelânea de estudos a Joaquim de Carvalho*, ed. Manuel Montezuma de Carvalho (Figueira da Foz, 1959-60), pp. 495-517. See also below, no. 239, pp. 186-240.
Review:
.1. Harvey Johnson, 'Gil Vicente in Portugal', *BCom*, XIII, 2 (Fall 1961), 9.

237　——. *Gil Vicente e a cidade de Lisboa.* Lisboa: Livraria Portugal, 1968. 128 pp.
Originally published in the *Boletim Cultural da Junta Distrital de Lisboa*, 65-6 (1966), 157-232; 67-8 (1967), 227-74.

238　——. *Gil Vicente e a evolução do teatro. Conferência pronunciada no Colégio Andrade Corvo de Torres Novas.* Lisboa: Minerva, 1965. 72 pp.

Review:
.1. A. Veloso, *Brotéria*, LXXXVIII (1969), 141.

239 —. *Gil Vicente e o teatro moderno: tentativa de esquematização da obra vicentina.* Lisboa: Minerva, 1965. 244 pp.
Review:
.1.A. Veloso, *Brotéria*, LXXXV (1968), 266.

240 —. *Gil Vicente, mestre do teatro simbólico-alegórico.* Lisboa: 1966. 30 pp.
(From *CNA, Órgão de divulgação e cultura dos Colégios de Nun'Alvares de Tomar*)

241 Carvalho, António Lopes de. *Gil Vicente. Guimarães, sua terra natal.* Guimarães: Câmara Municipal, 1959. 115 pp.
(2nd ed., 1961)
Reviews:
.1. L.C., *Ocidente*, LVII (1959), 152.
.2. A.A. Dória, *GilV*, XV (1964), 32.

242 Carvalho, Joaquim de. *Os sermões de Gil Vicente e a arte de pregar.* Lisboa: Revista Ocidente, 1948. 83 pp.
Reprinted in his *Estudos sobre a cultura portuguesa do século XVI*, II (Coimbra: Acta Universitatis Conimbrigensis, 1948), pp. 205-350. Pp. 345-50: Apêndice: 'Sobre as fontes do *Auto de Mofina Mendes*'. See Révah's reaction below, no. 287.

243 Castro Guimarães, Horácio de. *A sátira vicentina. Conferência pronunciada no Salão de Festas da Casa do Minho, em Lisboa, na noite de 12 de fevereiro de 1958, num Serão vicentino promovido pela Academia Portuguesa de Ex-Libris.* Vila do Conde: Escola Profissional de Santa Clara, 1958. 42 pp.
(From *Boletim da Academia Portuguesa de Ex-Libris*, 8-9)
Reviews:
.1. Anon., *Ocidente*, LV (1958), 214.
.2. M.C.A., *Brotéria*, LXIX (1959), 370.

244 Círculo de Cultura Teatral. *Comemoração do V centenário de Gil Vicente.* Porto: Livraria Divulgação, 1965. 77 pp.
Includes: António José Saraiva, 'Gil Vicente e Bertolt Brecht: o papel da ficção na descoberta da realidade', pp. 5-11 (see below, no. 363). Deniz-Jacinto, 'Prólogo para um espetáculo de Gil Vicente', pp. 13-14. The texts of *Auto da feira* (pp. 17-37), *Auto da Índia* (pp. 39-51), and *Auto de moralidade da Barca do Inferno* (pp. 53-77).
Review:
.1. A.R., *Brotéria*, LXXXI (1965), 713.

245 Clemente, Alice Rodrigues. "The Allegories of Gil Vicente." Dissertation, Brown University, 1967. 188 pp.
See *DA*, XXVIII (1967-8), 3138A.

246 Conde Júnior, B. Guerra. *Mestre Gil, fabricante de sonhos. O romance da vida de Gil Vicente*. Figueira da Foz: Edições Veneza, 1969. 191 pp.

247 Costa e Sá, Raul da. *Influência do elemento afro-negro na obra de Gil Vicente*. São Paulo: Saraiva, 1948. 188 pp.

248* D'Ans, A. "Contribution à la connaissance de l'oeuvre théâtrale de Gil Vicente." Dissertation, Université de Liège, 1960.

249 Dias, Jaime Lopes. *A Beira Baixa e o seu teatro popular na obra de Gil Vicente*. Lisboa: Academia das Ciências, 1959. 31 pp.
From *Memórias da Academia das Ciências de Lisboa, Classe de Letras*, VII (1959), 7-53.
Review:
.1. Aníbal Pinto de Castro, *RPF*, XI (1961), 226-7.

250 Elías de Tejada Spínola, Francisco. *As idéias políticas de Gil Vicente*. Trans. Manoel de Bettencourt e Galvão. Lisboa: Pro Domo, 1945. 119 pp.
Translation of his *Las ideas políticas de Gil Vicente* (Madrid, 1944).
Review:
.1. Luís Cabral de Moncada (see below, no. 342).

251 Gomes, A. Sousa. *Gil Vicente, artista multiforme*. Lisboa: Tip. Primorosa, 1968. 36 pp.

252 Gomes, Torquato. *Uma fala de Gil Vicente urdida por Torquato Gomes e endereçada aos portugueses de Moçambique no sarau evocativo do IV centenário do poeta, celebrado na cidade de Lourenço Marques aos XIII dias de novembro de MCMXXXVII*. Leiria, 1950. 31 pp.
Review:
.1. João Maia, *Brotéria*, LII (1951), 380.

253 —. *Visitação de Gil Vicente à cidade de Lisboa no quadragésimo ano da revolução nacional*. Braga: Livraria Cruz, 1967. 46 pp.

254 Gonçalves, Luiz da Cunha. *Gil Vicente e os homens do fôro*. 2nd ed. Lisboa: Ática, 1953. 50 pp.
(First ed., 1938)

255 Gonçalves, Sofia. *Auxiliar de interpretação do "Auto da Alma"*. Porto: Livraria Avis, 1963. 30 pp.

256 Hamilton-Faria, Hope. *The Farces of Gil Vicente: A Study in the Stylistics of Satire*. Madrid: Plaza Mayor, 1976. 138 pp.
Originally her dissertation for the University of Colorado (1974). See *DAI*, XXXV (1974-5), 7866A. *Contents:* Introduction. Synopses (*Farsa dos físicos, Quem tem farelos?, Auto de Inês Pereira, O Juiz da*

Beira, Romagem de agravados). Morphology of Satire. Language Realism. Satiric Style. Conclusion.

257 Janeiro, Armando Martins. *O teatro de Gil Vicente e o teatro clássico japonês*. Lisboa: Portugália Editora, 1967. 279 pp.
Part I: Teatro clássico japonês e teatro ocidental. O *Nô* e a sua origem religiosa—O *Kyogen*—O *Kabuki*—O teatro de bonecos. O drama europeu e a liturgia—Os *mistérios* e as *moralidades*—A farsa. Estética teatral na Europa medieval e no Japão. Gil Vicente, dramaturgo cíclico da Idade Media. Teatro vicentino, Teatro moderno e Antiteatro. O destino do homem no teatro vicentino. O teatro vicentino e o teatro clássico japonês. Teatro e poesia. *Part II*: Portuguese translations of six *Nô* and three *Kyogen* plays. See also: Armando Martins Janeiro, 'O teatro de Gil Vicente e o teatro clássico japonês', *Boletim da Sociedade de Geografia de Lisboa*, LXXXIV (1966), 323-58 (pp. 343-55 were reprinted, with additional material, as 'O teatro vicentino e o teatro clássico japonês' in *Ocidente*, LXXI (1966), 165-84. See also below, nos 326, 548.
Review:
.1. Teolinda Gersão Moreno, *Colóquio*, 47 (February 1968), 79.

258 Joiner, Ida Virginia. "The Dramatic Art of Gil Vicente." Dissertation, University of Texas, Austin, 1940. 249 pp.

259 Keates, Laurence W. *The Court Theatre of Gil Vicente*. Lisboa: Livraria Escolar, 1962. 154 pp.
Originally his M.A. thesis for the University of Birmingham, 1959. *Contents*: Gil Vicente at Court. Vicente's Cultural Background. Theatrical and Proto-theatrical Background. Vicente the Impresario. A Brief Analysis of Vicentine Theatre. Conclusion and Observations.

260 Köhler, Rudolf. *Der Einfluss Gil Vicentes auf das spanische Theater des Goldenen Zeitalters*. Dissertation, Georg-August Universität, Göttingen, 1968. v + 312 pp.
Review:
.1. Charlotte Stern, *HR*, XL (1972), 220-2.

261 Láfer, Celso. *O judeu em Gil Vicente*. São Paulo: Conselho Estadual de Cultura, 1963. 115 pp.
Reviews:
.1. N. Novaes Coelho, *Alfa*, 4 (1963), 222-5.
.2. Harvey L. Johnson, *Hispania*, XLVIII (1965), 177.
.3. João Maia, *Brotéria*, LXXX (1965), 546-7.

262 Lucas, João de Almeida. *Notas para uma edição de Gil Vicente: "Auto da Mofina Mendes"*. Lisboa: União Gráfica, 1942. 15 pp.

263 Lunardini, Peter John. "The Poetic Technique of Gil Vicente." Dissertation, University of New Mexico, 1953. 316 pp.

264 Marques, Amândio. *Gil Vicente beirão, nasceu em Guimarães de Tavares*. Porto: Casa de Beira Alta, 1966. 64 pp.

265* Matos Sequeira, Gustavo de. *Tomar e Gil Vicente*. Porto, 1960.

266 Megenney, William W. "A Study of Some of Gil Vicente's Aspects as a Didactic Moralist." M.A. thesis, University of New Mexico, 1966. 105 pp.

267 Michaëlis de Vasconcelos, Carolina. *Notas vicentinas: preliminares duma edição crítica das obras de Gil Vicente (Notas I a V)*. 2nd ed. Lisboa: Revista Ocidente, 1949. 661 pp.
   The first four *Notas* were published previously in the *Revista da Universidade de Coimbra*, I (1912), 205-93; VI (1918), 263-303; VII (1919), 25-61; IX (1925), 1-394. All five *Notas*, before being issued as a book, appeared in *Ocidente*, XXII (1944), 17-32, 265-96, 393-400; XXIII (1944), 33-48, 174-6, 257-88, 369-84; XXIV (1944), 33-47, 129-44, 225-40, 321-36; XXV (1945), 33-48, 129-44, 185-200, 281-96; and in the following Supplements: XXVI (1945), 261-324; XXVII (1945), 325-88; XXVIII (1946), 389-452; XXIX (1946), 453-84; XXX (1946), 485-516; XXXI (1947), 517-64; XXXII (1947), 565-609. *Contents*: Preliminares duma edição crítica das obras de Gil Vicente (pp. 1-8). Nota vicentina I: Gil Vicente em Bruxelas (pp. 9-83). II: A Rainha velha e *O monólogo do vaqueiro* (pp. 85-123). III: 'Romance à morte del Rei Dom Manuel e à aclamação de Dom João Terceiro' (pp. 125-47). IV: Cultura intelectual e nobreza literária (pp. 149-507). V: Autos portugueses de Gil Vicente e da Escola Vicentina (pp. 509-609). See also below, no. 341.
   Reviews:
   .1. A. Coelho de Magalhães, *RdP*, XV (1950), 196-201.
   .2. Domingos Maurício, *Brotéria*, L (1950), 731.

268 Miller, Neil. *O elemento pastoril no teatro de Gil Vicente*. Porto: Inova, 1970. 187 pp.
   O estado actual dos estudos vicentinos. A literatura pastoril até ao século XVI. Precursores dramáticos castelhanos do teatro pastoril vicentino. Tipologia rústica vicentina. Algumas características típicas da vida rústica vicentina. A natureza em Gil Vicente. Conclusão.
   Reviews:
   .1. Evelina P.S. Verdelho, *RPF*, XV (1969-71), 689 [brief].
   .2. Mário Martins, *CoL*, 7 (May 1972), 92-3.

269 Morão Correia, Sebastião. *Gil Vicente: nacionalismo e universalismo na sua obra. Conferência proferida em Luanda integrada nas comemorações do V centenário do nascimento de Gil Vicente*. Luanda: Serviços de Publicação do Comissariado Provincial da M.P., 1965. 35 pp.

270 Moreira, Thiers Martins. *A arte-maior na poesia dramática de Gil Vicente*.

Rio de Janeiro: Faculdade Nacional de Filosofia, 1945. 135 pp.
His thesis for the Universidade do Brasil.

271   Moseley, William W. "An Etymological Vocabulary of the Spanish in the Works of Gil Vicente." Dissertation, University of New Mexico, 1954. 735 pp.
See *DA*, XV (1955), 119-20.

272   Nemésio, Vitorino. *Gil Vicente: floresta de enganos.* Lisboa: Inquérito, 1941. 78 pp.

273   Oliveira, Joaquim de. *Humanidade e grandeza do Velho da horta.* Lisboa: Revista Ocidente, 1964. 96 pp.
See also below, nos 705-6.

274   Parker, Jack Horace. *Gil Vicente.* Twayne's World Authors Series, XXIX. New York: Twayne Publishers, 1967. 169 pp.
The Dramatist Goldsmith. The Spanish Début. The Continuation of the Salamancan Tradition. The Moralities and the Mysteries. The Farces and the Comedies. The Plays of Chivalry. The Miscellaneous Works. Gil Vicente's Songs. Gil Vicente the Impresario. Limitations and Achievements.
Reviews:
  .1. H.W. Hilborn, *Canadian Modern Language Review*, XXIV (1968), 103-4.
  .2. E.P., *RdP*, XXXIII (1968), 400.
  .3. Gerald Moser, *Hispania*, LII (1969), 155-6.
  .4. Rodrigo Olaia, *Brotéria*, LXXXVIII (1969), 706.
  .5. Charlotte Stern, *HR*, XXXVIII (1970), 215-17.

275   Pavão, José de Almeida. *Gil Vicente, poeta.* Ponta Delgada: Papelaria Âmbar, 1963. 191 pp.
Review:
  .1. A.C., *Ocidente*, LXVIII (1965), 46.

276*   Pech, Marie-Claude. "La Poésie lyrique castillane dans le théâtre de Gil Vicente." Dissertation, Université de Toulouse, 1967.

277   Pestana, Sebastião. *Estudos gil-vicentinos.* 2 vols. Sá da Bandeira, Angola. Tip. Imprex, 1972-5. 255, 264 pp.
Miscellany of generally short commentaries, by and large philological, on Gil Vicente's works. Vol. I has 50 commentaries, vol. II has 37. A third volume is scheduled to follow. See also below, no. 650.

278   —. *Gil Vicente em face de epopéia. Lição proferida na sessão inaugural do 5º curso de portugalidade que funcionou em Sá da Bandeira.* Sá da Bandeira, Angola, 1968. 32 pp.

279*   Pina, Luís de. *Pecado, culpa e angústia na cena gil-vicentina.* Porto, 1958.
(From *Revista de Guimarães* and *Gil Vicente*)

280   Pires, António. *Gil Vicente, poeta de Nossa Senhora*. Lisboa: Edições
       Letras e Artes, 1941. 47 pp.

281   Pratt, Óscar de. *Gil Vicente: notas e comentários*. 2nd ed. Lisboa: A.M.
       Teixeira, 1970. 286 pp.
       (First ed., 1931)
       Review:
       .1. A.F.G. Bell, *RFE*, XIX (1932), 84-5.

282   *Programa das comemorações do V centenário de Gil Vicente*. Lisboa:
       Ministério de Educação Nacional, 1965. 48 pp.

283   Quintela, Paulo. *As Barcas de Gil Vicente*. Lisboa, 1943. 31 pp.
       (From *RFLUL*, IX)

284   *V centenário de Gil Vicente. Programa da semana de teatro vicentino
       (29 de novembro a 4 de dezembro)*. Lisboa: Ministério de Educação
       Nacional, 1965. 45 pp.

285   Raposo, M.F. Bastos. *Nota sobre Gil Vicente*. Coimbra: Gráfica de
       Coimbra, 1949. 14 pp. (2nd ed., 1955)
       (From *Estudos, Órgão do C.A.D.C.*)

285A   Reckert, Stephen. *Gil Vicente: espíritu y letra*. I: *Estudios*. Madrid:
       Gredos, 1977. 484 pp.
       Includes revised and expanded versions of nos 357 (pp. 171-94), 358
       (pp. 197-223), 421 (the part on the *Barcas*—pp. 60-101), 603 (pp. 135-
       70), 654 (pp. 224-35). *Contents*: Prólogo. Gil Vicente. Teatro de van-
       guardia en el siglo XVI. Forma interior del drama vicentino: las *Barcas*.
       El drama doble de las tres potencias del Alma. La lírica vicentina:
       estructura y estilo. "Bajo el signo del latín" (Cultura literaria de Gil
       Vicente). El verdadero texto de las ediciones primitivas. Marginalia
       vicentina (tres apostillas). La problemática textual de *Don Duardos*.
       Vol. II will include a critical edition of *Dom Duardos* and Gil Vicente's
       complete poetry.
       Reviews:
       .1. John Lihani, *Hispania*, LXI (1978), 559.
       .2. R. Clive Willis, *BHS*, LV (1978), 275.
       .3. José Antonio Míguez, *Arbor*, XCVII (1977), 435-8.

286   Révah, I.S. *Deux "autos" de Gil Vicente restitués à leur auteur. Lições
       proferidas em 20 e 27 de maio de 1948*. Lisboa: Academia das Ciências,
       1949. 79 pp.
       (*Obra da geração humana* and *Auto de Deus Padre e Justiça e Misericórdia*).
       Reviews:
       .1. A.J. da Costa Pimpão, *Biblos*, XXIV (1948), 571-4 [Révah responds
           to the reviewer's arguments in 'L'Attribution à Gil Vicente de
           la *Obra da geração humana*.' *BHTP*, I (1950), 93-116. Costa

Pimpão objects in 'Em torno de uma portada,' *Biblos*, XXV (1949), 439-44. Révah argues again in 'À propos d'une nouvelle note du Prof. A.J. da Costa Pimpão,' *BHTP*, II (1951), 89-106, and Costa Pimpão counterattacks in 'A propósito da atribuição de dois autos de autor ou autores desconhecidos a Gil Vicente,' *Biblos*, XXVI (1950), 520-36. The two articles by Costa Pimpão are reprinted in no. 317, below].

.2. Eugenio Asensio, *RFE*, XXXIII (1949), 409-14.

.3. Georges Le Gentil, *BH*, LI (1949), 63-6.

.4. A.J. Saraiva, *Portucale*, XXII (1949), 277-9.

.5. Marcel Bataillon, *RPhi*, III (1949-50), 319-22.

.6. Aubrey F.G. Bell, *BAbr*, XXIV (1950), 47; and *HR*, XVIII (1950), 348-50.

.7. Joseph E. Gillet, *RR*, XLI (1950), 216-18.

.8. U.T. Holmes, *Hispania*, XXXIII (1950), 182-3.

.9. A.R. Nykl, *MLN*, LXV (1950), 275.

.10. Robert Ricard, *RHTh*, II (1950), 94-5.

.11. Gomes de Zurara, *Brotéria*, L (1950), 591-2.

287 —. *Les Sermons de Gil Vicente: en marge d'un opuscule du professeur Joaquim de Carvalho*. Lisboa: Ottosgráfica, 1949. 62 pp.
For Carvalho's work, see above, no. 242.
Reviews:

.1. Georges Le Gentil, *BH*, LI (1949), 66.

.2. A.J. Saraiva, *Portucale*, XXII (1949), 279-80.

.3. Marcel Bataillon, *RPhi*, III (1949-50), 322.

.4. Aubrey F.G. Bell, *HR*, XVIII (1950), 348-50.

.5. Joseph E. Gillet, *RR*, XLI (1950), 217.

.6. U.T. Holmes, *Hispania*, XXXIII (1950), 182-3.

.7. Domingos Maurício, *Brotéria*, L (1950), 163.

.8. A.R. Nykl, *MLN*, LXV (1950), 276.

.9. Robert Ricard, *RHTh*, II (1950), 95.

288 Riggio, Edward Anthony. "The Place of the Comic in the Theater of Gil Vicente." Dissertation, University of Pittsburgh, 1969. 677 pp.
See *DAI*, XXX (1969-70), 1572A.

289 Sampaio, Joaquim Augusto Cardoso. *Palestra sobre Gil Vicente pronunciada no Colégio de Via Sacra.* Seia: Tip. Montes Hermínios, 1949. 12 pp. (From *A Voz da Serra*)

290* Santiago, Rui Protásio. *Provérbios na obra de Gil Vicente*. Lisboa: Liceu de Gil Vicente, 1941.

291 Saraiva, António José. *Gil Vicente e o fim do teatro medieval.* 3rd ed. Lisboa: Europa-América, 1970. 213 pp.
First ed., 1942; second, 1965. Originally his dissertation for the

Universidade de Lisboa. *Part I*: Sobre o sentido da evolução do teatro medieval (A evolução dos géneros. O teatro na evolução da arte medieval). *Part II*: Gil Vicente (Os géneros. Vestígios do simbolismo litúrgico em Gil Vicente e tentativa pessoal de arranjo segundo uma nova unidade. Os tipos de Gil Vicente e os quadros em que se exibem. Inexistência da unidade dramática em Gil Vicente. Tentativa de simbolismo por meio do teatro alegórico. O simbolismo pela antinomia dos dois mundos). *Part III*: Considerações em torno do teatro calderoniano. *Apêndice* sobre os precedentes do teatro de Gil Vicente.

Reviews:
.1.   D.M. Gomes dos Santos, *Brotéria*, XXXVIII (1944), 308-18.
.2.   Charles V. Aubrun, *BH*, XLIX (1947), 467-8.
.3.   Marcel Bataillon, *Revue de Littérature Comparée*, XXII (1948), 135-9.
.4.   Osvaldo Aguiar, *Rumo*, 110 (April 1966), 314-15.
.5.   João Mendes, *Brotéria*, LXXXII (1966), 676-83.
.6.   G.M. Moser, *Hispania*, XLIX (1966), 886.

292   Sletsjøe, Leif. *O elemento cénico em Gil Vicente*. Lisboa: Casa Portuguesa, 1965. 151 pp.
Introdução ao teatro de Gil Vicente. As várias "fases" da obra teatral vicentina. Classificação das peças, e justificação dela. A trajectória vicentina, e a evolução posterior. *Anexo*: As sinopses "cénicas" das peças. Epílogo.

Reviews:
.1.   J. Pinharanda Gomes, *Ocidente*, LXXI (1966), 292.
.2.   Holger Sten, *StN*, XXXVIII (1966), 353-5.
.3.   Thomas R. Hart, *MLN*, LXXXIII (1968), 351-2.

293   Teyssier, Paul. *La Langue de Gil Vicente*. Paris: Klincksieck, 1959. 554 pp.
Originally his dissertation for the Sorbonne (1956). *Contents:* Introduction. Note préliminaire. Le sayagais. La langue rustique portugaise. Les commères. Les juifs. Nègres, maures et tziganes. Langues étrangères: français et italien. Le système bilingue de Gil Vicente. Influence du portugais sur l'espagnol. De quelques procédés spéciaux. Une forêt de symboles. 'Tan dulce retórica y escogido estilo'. La veine populaire. Conclusion. Bibliographie.

Reviews:
.1.   Luciana Stegagno Picchio, 'Questioni gilvicentine', *CN*, XIX (1959), 265-74 [review article; see below, no. 369].
.2.   H. Kröll, *RJ*, XI (1960), 418-22.
.3.   Silveira Bueno, *Jornal de Filologia*, 1-2 (1960-1), 65-9.
.4.   Thomas R. Hart, *MLN*, LXXVI (1961), 181-5.

.5.   P. Pohl, *RF*, LXXIII (1961), 441-5.
.6.   Charlotte Stern, *HR*, XXIX (1961), 269-73.
.7.   T.P. Waldron, *BHS*, XXXVIII (1961), 247-9.
.8.   Frida Weber de Kurlat, *Filología*, VII (1961), 211-18.
.9.   A.J. da Costa Pimpão, *Revista de História Literária de Portugal*, I (1962), 322-9.
.10. Leif Sletsjøe, *StN*, XXXIV (1962), 187-92.
.11. José Joaquín Montes G., *Thesaurus: Boletín del Instituto Caro y Cuervo*, XVIII (1963), 511-15.
.12. J.G. Herculano de Carvalho, *RPhi*, XVII (1963-4), 809-13.

294   Tomé, José Ferreira. *Duas fases na vida de Gil Vicente (ourives até 1506, poeta desde 1502): subsídios para a sua identificação*. Lisboa: Tip. Americana, 1947. 83 pp. + plates.
First ed., 1938. The author has collected a large number of technical terms from 28 of Gil Vicente's plays to support his identification of the dramatist with the goldsmith.

295   Tomlins, Jack E. "The Nature of Gil Vicente's Dramatic Artistry." Dissertation, Princeton University, 1957. 140 pp.
See *DA*, XVIII (1958), 238.

296* **Ventura, Augusta Faria Gersão.** *Elementos astronómicos das obras de Gil Vicente e de Camões*. Lisboa: União Gráfica, 1941.
(From *Liceus de Portugal*, 2-4, 1940-1)

297   Vieira, M. Higino. *Crítica social de Gil Vicente, através da farsa "Quem tem farelos?"*. Porto: Empresa Industrial Gráfica, 1941. 36 pp.
Reprinted from *Portucale*, XIII (1940), 86-94, 142-52, 199-202; XIV (1941), 26-8, 82-5, 147-52.

298   Vitor, Edgar d'Almeida. *Gil Vicente, um espírito entre duas épocas*. Belém: Centro de Estudos Luso-Brasileiros, Faculdade de Filosofia da Universidade Federal do Pará, 1970 (?). 32 pp.

299   Zuquete, Afonso. *Idéias médicas de Gil Vicente*. Porto: Tip. Costa Carregal, 1944. 22 pp.
(From *Jornal do Médico*. On the *Farsa dos físicos*)

B. Chapters in books and essays in collections

300   Alonso, Dámaso. 'El hidalgo Camilote y el hidalgo Don Quijote'. In his *Del Siglo de Oro a este siglo de siglas*. 2nd ed. Madrid: Gredos, 1968, pp. 20-8.
Appeared first in *RFE*, XX (1933), 391-7; XXI (1934), 283-4.

301   —. 'La poesía dramática en la *Tragicomedia de Don Duardos*'. In his *Ensayos sobre poesía española*. Madrid: Revista de Occidente, 1944, pp. 125-44.

302   —. *Obras completas*. II: *Estudios y ensayos sobre literatura. Primera parte: Desde los orígenes románicos hasta finales del siglo XVI*. Madrid: Gredos, 1973.

Includes: 'Poesías de Gil Vicente' (pp. 461-4): originally served as prologue to his edition of *Poesías de Gil Vicente* in *Cruz y Raya*, 10 (1934), 115-18, and later in a new edition of the same (México: Séneca, 1940). Was again reprinted in his *De los siglos oscuros al de Oro* (Madrid: Gredos, 1958), pp. 148-52. 'Un lusismo de Gil Vicente' (pp. 469-74): published in *RFE*, XXIV (1937), 208-13, and reprinted in *De los siglos oscuros*, pp. 158-64. 'Tres procesos de dramatización' (pp. 475-78): published in the *Revista Nacional de Educación*, III (1943), 34-7, and reprinted in *De los siglos oscuros*, pp. 144-47 (on Gil Vicente and Lope de Vega). 'Juan Fernández de Heredia en la tradición peninsular' (pp. 479-90): published in *De los siglos oscuros*, pp. 165-77 (a comparison of the Valencian's theater with that of Gil Vicente and Torres Naharro).

303   Asensio, Eugenio. *Estudios portugueses*. Introduction by José V. de Pina Martins. Paris: Fundação Calouste Gulbenkian—Centro Cultural Português, 1974.

Includes: 'De los momos cortesanos a los autos caballerescos de Gil Vicente' (pp. 25-36): from *Anais do Primeiro Congresso Brasileiro da Língua Falada no Teatro* (Rio de Janeiro: Ministério da Educação e Cultura, 1958), pp. 163-72. 'Las fuentes de las *Barcas* de Gil Vicente. lógica intelectual e imaginación dramática' (pp. 59-77): from *BHTP*, IV (1953), 207-37. 'El *Auto dos Quatro Tempos* de Gil Vicente' (pp. 79-101): from *RFE*, XXXIII (1949), 350-75.

Review:

.1.   José Ares Montes, *Ínsula*, 354 (May 1976), 15.

304   —. 'Gil Vicente y las cantigas paralelísticas "restauradas". ¿Folclore o poesía original?' In his *Poética y realidad en el cancionero peninsular de la Edad Media*. 2nd ed. Madrid: Gredos, 1970, pp. 134-76. (First ed., 1957)

Reviews:

.1.   Albin Eduard Beau, *BdF*, XVI (1956-7), 398-401.
.2.   Domingos Maurício, *Brotéria*, LXVII (1958), 327-9.
.3.   I.S. Révah, *BEP*, XXI (1958), 313-15.
.4.   J.M. Santano, *Archivum*, VIII (1958), 326-8.
.5.   Juan Villegas Morales, *Anales de la Universidad de Chile*, CXVI (1958), 151-3.
.6.   Manuel José Bayo, *CH*, 112 (April 1959), 68-70.
.7.   María Soledad Carrasco Urgoiti, *RHM*, XXV (1959), 246.
.8.   Enrique Moreno Báez, *Ínsula*, 150 (15 May 1959), 7.
.9.   Edwin B. Place, *Speculum*, XXXIV (1959), 248-50.
.10.   C.C. Smith, *BHS*, XXXVI (1959), 62-3.

.11. Luciana Stegagno Picchio, *CN*, XIX (1959), 147-50.
.12. Pierre Groult, *LR*, XIV (1960), 155-7.
.13. John E. Keller, *BAbr*, XXXIV (1960), 128.
.14. Lawrence B. Kiddle, *RR*, LI (1960), 215-16.
.15. Ruth House Webber, *HR*, XXIX (1961), 335-8.
.16. Elias L. Rivers, *MLN*, LXXXVI (1971), 302.

305 Bataillon, Marcel. 'Une source de Gil Vicente et de Montemôr: la Méditation de Savonarole sur le *Miserere*.' In his *Études sur le Portugal au temps de l'humanisme*. Coimbra: Acta Universitatis Conimbrigensis, 1952, pp. 197-217.
Reprinted from *BEP*, III (1936), 1-16.
Reviews (of the book):
.1. I.S. Révah, *BEP*, XVI (1952), 236-9.
.2. H. Bernard-Maître, *AHSI*, XXII (1953), 599-601.
.3. J. Cruz Costa, *RdH*, VI (1953), 505-6.
.4. T.H. Donghi, *Imago Mundi*, 1 (September 1953), 79-80.
.5. N.J. Lamb, *BHS*, XXX (1953), 118-19.
.6. L. de Matos, *BII*, LV (1953), 393-5.
.7. G.M. Bertini, *QIA*, II (1953-4), 451-4.
.8. María Rosa Lida de Malkiel, *RPhi*, VII (1953-4), 254-6.
.9. Gerald M. Moser, *HR*, XXII (1954), 237.
.10. A.E. Beau, *RF*, LXVI (1955), 201-11.
.11. E. Gianturco, *BAbr*, XXIX (1955), 62.

306 Beau, Albin Eduard. *Estudos*. Vol. I. Coimbra: Acta Universitatis Conimbrigensis, 1959, pp. 73-347.
Contains the following: 'Gil Vicente: o aspecto "medieval" e "renascentista" da sua obra,' pp. 73-158: first published in *BdF*, IV (1936), 358-80 and V (1937), 93-114, 257-76. 'As *Barcas* de Gil Vicente', pp. 159-218: first appeared as 'Die *Barcas* des Gil Vicente,' in *RF*, LIII (1939), 300-55. 'A música na obra de Gil Vicente', pp. 219-49: originally published as 'Die Musik im Werk des Gil Vicente,' in *VKR*, IX (1936), 177-201, and subsequently in Portuguese, *Biblos*, XIV (1938), 329-55. 'Gil Vicente na Alemanha,' pp. 251-347: from the *Boletim do Instituto Alemão*, IX (1939), 69-159.
Reviews:
.1. I.S. Révah, *BEP*, XXII (1959-60), 285-7.
.2. W. Mettmann, *ASNSL*, CXCVII (1960), 94.
.3. P. Lidmilová, *PP*, VI (1963), 333-4.

307 ——. 'Sobre el bilingüismo en Gil Vicente.' In *Studia philologica: homenaje ofrecido a Dámaso Alonso por sus amigos y discípulos*. Vol. I. Madrid: Gredos, 1960, pp. 217-24.

308 Beleza, José Manuel Merêa Pizarro. 'A propósito da "cena do enforcado" no *Auto da Barca do Inferno* de Gil Vicente.' In *Colóquio internacional*

comemorativo do centenário da abolição da pena de morte em Portugal (Universidade de Coimbra, 1967). Coimbra: Gráfica de Coimbra, 1968. Vol. I, pp. 397-407.

308A Bell, Aubrey FitzGerald. 'Gil Vicente.' In his *Studies in Portuguese Literature*. New York: Gordon Press, 1975, pp. 55-80. Reprint of the 1914 ed. (Oxford: B.H. Blackwell).

309* Berardinelli, Cleonice. 'Gil Vicente e o teatro pré-vicentino em Portugal.' In her *De literatura portuguêsa*. Rio de Janeiro: Grifo, 1974.

310 Bertini, Giovanni Maria. *Il teatro spagnolo del primo rinascimento seguito da uno studio su "Lazarillo de Tormes".* Lezioni raccolte dal Dr Giulio Pulliero nel corso tenuto dal Prof. G.M. Bertini a Ca'Foscari nell'anno accademico 1945-46. Venezia: F. Montuoro, 1946.
Study of Gil Vicente on pp. 159-97. See also following entry.

311 —. *Teatro spagnolo del primo rinascimento: Juan del Encina, Gil Vicente, Bartolomé de Torres Naharro.* Venezia: Già Zanetti, 1945. 270 pp.

312 Bowra, C.M. 'The Songs of Gil Vicente.' In his *Inspiration and Poetry*. London: Macmillan, 1955, pp. 90-111.
Reprinted from *Atlante*, I (1953), 3-21.
Reviews:
.1. Anon., *TLS* (17 June 1955), 334.
.2. William Barrett, *The New York Times* (14 August 1955), 4.
.3. Geoffrey Brereton, *New Stateman and Nation* (2 July 1955), 18.
.4. David Daiches, *Manchester Guardian* (28 June 1955), 6.
.5. Donat O'Donnell, *Spectator* (8 July 1955), 53.
.6. H. Peschmann, *English*, X (1955), 230-1.
.7. H.G. Porteus, *Time and Tide* (18 June 1955), 806.
.8. Yakov Malkiel, *RPhi*, IX (1955-6), 267-8.
.9. Bernard Gicovate, *Comparative Literature*, VIII (1956), 168-70.
.10. M. Jarrett-Kerr, *Essays in Criticism*, VI (1956), 78-87.

313 Castro e Almeida, Virgínia de. 'Gil Vicente.' In *Grandes portugueses*. IV. Lisboa: Secretariado de Propaganda Nacional, 1945. 28 pp.

313A Cidade, Hernâni. 'O teatro vicentino.' In his *Luís de Camões*. III: *Os autos e o teatro do seu tempo; as cartas e seu conteúdo biográfico.* Lisboa: Livraria Bertrand, 1956, pp. 1-58.
Reviews:
.1. Damien Saunal, *BEP*, XIX (1955-6), 223-5.
.2. Gerald M. Moser, *HR*, XXV (1957), 307-8.
.3. Domingos Maurício, *Brotéria,* LXIV (1957), 243-4.

314 Cintra, Luís Filipe Lindley. 'Tratamento de intimidade e tratamento de cortesia nas obras de Gil Vicente.' In his *Sobre "formas de tratamento" na língua portuguesa*. Lisboa: Livros Horizonte, 1972, pp. 43-73.

Originally the "comunicação apresentada no Simpósio Vicentino, reunido em Lisboa, na Faculdade de Letras, em 1965, a fim de celebrar o V centenário de Gil Vicente."

315   Clemente, Alice R. *'Comédia sobre a divisa da cidade de Coimbra*: fantasía caballeresca.' In *Homenaje a William L. Fichter: Estudios sobre el teatro antiguo hispánico y otros ensayos.* Ed. A. David Kossoff & José Amor y Vázquez, Madrid: Castalia, 1971, pp. 161-74.

> *Reviews* (of the book):
> .1. Jennifer Lowe, *MLR*, LXVIII (1973), 668-70.
> .2. Otis H. Green, *HR*, XLII (1974), 448-56.
> .3. Alan K.G. Paterson, *BHS*, LI (1974), 385-7.
> .4. Antonio Rey, *Segismundo*, 19-20 (1974), 361-5.

316   Corbin, Solange. 'Les Textes musicaux de l'*Auto da Alma* (Identification d'une pièce citée par Gil Vicente).' In *Mélanges d'histoire du Moyen Âge, dédiés à la memoire de Louis Halphen.* Paris: PUF, 1951, pp. 137-43.

317   Costa Pimpão, Álvaro Júlio da. *Escritos diversos.* Coimbra: Acta Universitatis Conimbrigensis, 1972.

Includes: 'Em torno de uma portada' (pp. 63-72). from *Biblos*, XXV (1949), 439-44. 'A propósito da atribuição de dois autos de autor ou autores desconhecidos a Gil Vicente' (pp. 73-96): from *Biblos*, XXVI (1950), 520-36. 'Estética e geografia. Nótula a propósito de um artigo sobre Gil Vicente, beirão' (pp. 97-109): from *Biblos*, XIX (1943), 483-91. 'As correntes dramáticas na literatura portuguesa do século XVI' (pp. 413-43): from *A evolução e o espírito do teatro em Portugal. 2º ciclo (1ª série) de conferências promovido pelo "Século"* (Lisboa: "O Século", 1947), pp. 133-68. The first two essays attack Révah's attribution of the *Obra da geração humana* and *Auto de Deus Padre* to Gil Vicente (see above, no. 286). The third refutes the claim made by Valentim da Silva, in 'Gil Vicente, beirão,' *Beira Alta*, II, 1 (1943), that the dramatist was a native of Guimarães de Tavares.

318   —. 'Gil Vicente.' In *Os grandes portugueses.* Ed. Hernâni Cidade. Vol. I. Lisboa: Arcádia, [1960], pp. 355-67.

319   Cunha, Celso Ferreira da. 'Regularidade e irregularidade na versificação do primeiro auto das *Barcas* de Gil Vicente.' In his *Língua e verso. Ensaios.* 2nd ed. Rio de Janeiro: Livraria São José, 1968, pp. 49-76.

Reprinted from *Studia philologica: homenaje ofrecido a Dámaso Alonso por sus amigos y discípulos.* Vol. I. Madrid: Gredos, 1960, pp. 459-79.

> *Review* (of the book):
> .1. Manuel de Paiva Boléo, *RPF*, XV (1969-71), 501-2 [brief mention].

320   Emerenciano, Jordão. 'A hora de Gil Vicente.' In *Actas do V Colóquio*

Internacional de Estudos Luso-brasileiros (Coimbra, 1963). Vol. III. Coimbra: Universidade, 1965, pp. 513-27.

In a highly patriotic tone, he describes Gil Vicente's Portugal politically, socially and culturally.

321 Frèches, Claude-Henri. 'Origines et tendances du théâtre de Gil Vicente.' In his *Le Théâtre neo-latin au Portugal (1550-1745).* Paris: Librairie A.G. Nizet, 1964, pp. 24-50.

Reviews (of the book):
.1. Luciana Stegagno Picchio, *CN*, XXIV (1964), 289-94 [see below, no. 369].
.2. Pierre Le Gentil, *BEP*, XXVI (1965), 250-3.
.3. Mário Martins, *Brotéria*, LXXX (1965), 261-3.
.4. Américo da Costa Ramalho, *Humanitas* (Coimbra), XVII-XVIII (1965-6), 361-3.
.5. Rainer Hess, *RF*, LXXVIII (1966), 618-19.
.6. Jean-Michel Massa, *RHTh*, XVIII (1966), 236-8.
.7. Joaquim Lourenço de Carvalho, *Euphrosyne*, I (1967), 291-2.
.8. M. Scaduto, *AHSI*, XXXVI (1967), 194-200.

322 Gerhardt, Mia I. 'La Génie de la pastorale nationale: Gil Vicente.' In her *La Pastorale. Essai d'analyse littéraire.* Assen: Van Gorcum, 1950, pp. 140-54.

Originally her dissertation for the University of Leiden: "Essai d'analyse littéraire de la Pastorale dans les littératures italienne, espagnole et française."

Reviews (of the book):
.1. Alexandre Micha, *Bibliothèque d'Humanisme et Renaissance*, XIII (1951), 117-20.
.2. A. Lytton Sells, *French Studies*, V (1951), 161-3.
.3. C. Serrurier, *Neophilologus*, XXXV (1951), 171-2.

323 Guimarães, Luiz de Oliveira. 'Gil Vicente inspirador dos *Lusíadas*.' In *Congresso do mundo português.* Lisboa: Comissão Executiva dos Centenários, 1940, vol. V, no. 3, pp. 449-57.

The author claims that Camões was inspired by the *Auto da Fama.*

324 Hathaway, Robert L. *Love in the Early Spanish Theatre.* Madrid: Plaza Mayor, 1975, pp. 120-41.

He discusses Gil Vicente's treatment of courtly love in the *Comédia do viúvo, Dom Duardos,* and *Amadis de Gaula.*

Reviews:
.1. Ruth Lundelius, *BCom*, XXVIII (1976), 53-4.
.2. David H. Darst, *Journal of Hispanic Philology*, I (1977-8), 158-9.

325 Isaza Calderón, Baltasar. *El retorno a la naturaleza: Los orígenes del tema y sus direcciones fundamentales en la literatura española.* 2nd ed. Madrid:

Industrias Gráficas España, 1966, pp. 106-18.
Gil Vicente's treatment of nature. The book was originally the author's dissertation for the Universidad de Madrid (1933), and was published for the first time in 1934.

326 Janeira, Armando Martins. *Japanese and Western Literature: A Comparative Study*. Rutland, Vermont &Tokyo: Charles E. Tuttle, 1970.
Ch. xvii: 'Japanese Classic Drama and European Mediaeval Drama.' On Gil Vicente, pp. 303-30. The author's earlier publications (nos 257, 548) appear under the name Janeiro.

327 Leal, César. *Os cavaleiros de Júpiter*. Recife: Universidade Federal de Pernambuco, 1969.
Ch. ii: 'Sôbre a poesia lírica e dramática de Gil Vicente', pp. 45-65. First published as 'Reflexões sôbre a poesia lírica e dramática de Gil Vicente,' in *Estudos Universitários*, VI (1966), 103-22, and subsequently in Leônidas Câmara, Renato Carneiro Campos and César Leal, *Três estudos literários* (Recife: Universidade Federal de Pernambuco, 1967).

328 Le Gentil, Pierre. 'Notes sur les compositions lyriques du théâtre de Gil Vicente.' In *Mélanges d'histoire du théâtre du Moyen Âge et de la Renaissance offerts à Gustave Cohen, Professeur Honoraire en Sorbonne, par ses collègues, ses élèves et ses amis*. Paris: Nizet, 1950, pp. 249-60.

329 Lida de Malkiel, María Rosa. 'Para la génesis del *Auto de la sibila Casandra.*' In her *Estudios de literatura española y comparada*. Buenos Aires: EUDEBA, 1966, pp. 157-72.
First published in *Filología*, V (1959), 47-63.

329A Lihani, John. 'Lucas Fernández and Gil Vicente.' In his *Lucas Fernández*. Twayne's World Authors Series, CCLI. New York: Twayne Publishers, 1973, pp. 40-9.

330 Livermore, Ann. 'Gil Vicente and Shakespeare.' In *Proceedings of the International Colloquium on Luso-Brazilian Studies (Washington, October 15-20, 1950)*. Nashville: Vanderbilt University Press, 1953, pp. 158-60. See also below, no. 549.

331 Lopes, Óscar. *Ler e depois: Crítica e interpretação literária*. I. 2nd ed. Porto: Inova, 1969.
Includes: 'O sem-sentido em Gil Vicente' (pp. 79-96): first published in *ESP SL*, 457 (4 December 1965), 1; and in *Seara Nova*, XLIV (1965), 275-8. 'Reflexão metodológica sobre "o sem-sentido em Gil Vicente" ' (pp. 97-112): reprinted from *Vértice*, XXV (1965), 807-16, where it appeared under the title 'Estrutura do cómico vicentino. Um aspecto: os parvos.'

332 Marbán, Edilberto. 'Gil Vicente, el magnífico.' In his *El teatro español medieval y del Renacimiento. Una obra para estudiantes de español*. New York: Las Américas, 1971, pp. 105-32.

333   Marques Braga, Manuel. 'Gil Vicente e a sociedade do seu tempo.' In *A evolução e o espírito do teatro em Portugal. 2º ciclo (1ª série) de conferências promovido pelo "Século".* Lisboa: "O Século", 1947, pp. 53-81.

334   Martins, Mário. 'Da glosa dos provérbios de Santilhana em Gil Vicente.' In his *Estudos de cultura medieval.* II. Braga: Edições Magnificat, 1972, pp. 33-8.

335   —. *Introdução histórica à vidência do tempo e da morte.* I: *Da destemporalização medieval até ao "Cancioneiro Geral" e a Gil Vicente.* Braga: Livraria Cruz, 1969.
    Ch. viii: 'Pranto vicentino à morte de D. Manuel I' (pp. 105-12). Ch. xiii: 'O Tempo e a Morte nos autos vicentinos' (pp. 213-36): from *Brotéria*, LXXXI (1965), 186-203. Ch. xiv: 'Gil Vicente e as figuras da Dança Macabra nos Livros de Horas' (pp. 237-95).
    Reviews:
    .1. N. da Fonte, *Ciudad de Dios*, CLXXXI (1969), 648-9.
    .2. A. Morão, *Brotéria*, LXXXIX (1969), 249-50.
    .3. J. Pinharanda Gomes, *Ocidente*, LXXIX (1970), 32-3.
    .4. José V. de Pina Martins, *Arquivos do Centro Cultural Português*, II (1970), 668-74.

336   McKendrick, Melveena. *Woman and Society in the Spanish Drama of the Golden Age: A Study of the "mujer varonil".* London: Cambridge University Press, 1974.
    Pp. 45-51 on Gil Vicente's *Auto da sibila Cassandra*, the first Spanish play "in which the theme of active feminism appears".
    Reviews:
    .1. A.V. Ebersole, *Hispania*, LVIII (1975), 979-80.
    .2. John G. Weiger, *BCom*, XXVII (1975), 141-6.
    .3. John Brotherton, *JAULLA*, 45 (1976), 136-7.
    .4. Enrique Canito, *Ínsula*, 354 (May 1976), 8-9.
    .5. Daniel Rogers, *MLR*, LXXI (1976), 447-8.
    .6. Frida Weber de Kurlat, *BHS*, LIV (1977), 61-3.

337   Meier, Harri. 'Gil Vicente als Dichter der portugiesischen Geschichte (Die *Comédia do viúvo*).' In *Portugal 1140-1640. Festschrift der Universität Köln zu den portugiesischen Staatsfeiern des Jahres 1940.* Köln: Balduin Pick, 1940, pp. 140-9.

338   —. 'Os dramas de Gil Vicente.' In his *Ensaios de filologia românica.* Lisboa: Revista de Portugal, 1948, pp. 235-9. 2nd ed. Rio de Janeiro: Grifo, 1973.

339   Mendes, João. 'O erasmismo de Gil Vicente.' In his *Monte Parnaso-Monte Carmelo. Ensaios.* Braga: Livraria Cruz, 1944, pp. 53-84.

He defends Gil Vicente's orthodoxy and denies that he was an Erasmian. See his 'Do erasmismo de Gil Vicente', *Brotéria*, XXIII (1936), 303-19.

340   Menéndez Pelayo, Marcelino. 'Gil Vicente.' In his *Antología de poetas líricos castellanos*. Ed. Enrique Sánchez Reyes. Vol. III. Madrid & Santander: CSIC, 1944, ch. xxvii, pp. 347-95.
This is vol. XIX of the *Edición Nacional de las Obras Completas de Menéndez Pelayo*, dir. Miguel Artigas. This essay was originally published in *Antología*, vol. VII, pp. clxiii-ccxxv (Madrid: Librería de Hernando, 1898).

341   Michaëlis de Vasconcelos, Carolina. 'Autos portugueses de Gil Vicente e da Escola Vicentina.' In her *Dispersos. Originais portugueses*. I: *Vária*. Lisboa: Revista Ocidente, 1969, pp. 209-99.
First appeared as Introduction to the facsimile edition of *Autos portugueses de Gil Vicente y de la escuela vicentina* (Madrid: Centro de Estudios Históricos, 1922), and later, as *Nota* V, in her *Notas vicentinas* (see above, no. 267).
Review (of the volume):
.1. M. Simões, *Brotéria*, XCII (1971), 849-50.

342   Moncada, Luís Cabral de. 'As idéias políticas de Gil Vicente.' In his *Estudos filosóficos e históricos: artigos, discursos, conferências e recenções críticas*. II. Coimbra: Acta Universitatis Conimbrigensis, 1959, pp. 484-92.
Review article on Francisco Elías de Tejada Spínola's *Las ideas políticas de Gil Vicente* (see above, no. 250). It was first published in the *Boletim da Faculdade de Direito da Universidade de Coimbra*, XX (1945).

343   Moseley, William W. 'Portugal and the Vision of Empire in Gil Vicente.' In *Interdisciplinary Essays*. III. Ed. Stephen H. Good & Olaf P. Tollefsen. Emmitsburg, Maryland: Mt St Mary's College, 1973, pp. 21-3.

344   Moser, Fernando de Mello. See 733.

344A   Nemésio, Vitorino. 'A campanha vicentina.' In *Afonso Lopes Vieira—In Memoriam*. Lisboa: Livraria Sá da Costa, 1947, pp. 165-9.

345   —. 'Dois homens do povo. II: Gil Vicente.' In his *Ondas médias: biografia e literatura*. Lisboa: Bertrand, [1945], pp. 67-74.

346   Osório, João de Castro. *O além-mar na literatura portuguesa. Época dos descobrimentos*. Lisboa: Edições Gama, 1948, pp. 169-265.
He discusses the influence of the sea and the overseas on Gil Vicente's work. Ch. vi: 'O reverso da grandeza humana da expansão marítima observado pelo génio cómico' (pp. 169-87). Ch. vii: 'O génio satírico recriado pelo julgamento de um aspecto social da expansão ultramarina' (pp. 189-211). Ch. viii: 'A expansão ultramarina e as raízes nacionais do pensamento dramático português' (pp. 213-34). Ch. ix: 'A visão épico-

dramática da expansão portuguesa e a primeira obra do novo pensamento humanista' (pp. 235-65).

347 Parker, Jack Horace. 'Gil Vicente's Contribution to the *Cancioneiro geral* (1516): His Intervention in the "Processo de Vasco Abul".' In *Homage to John M. Hill*. Ed. Walter Poesse. Bloomington: Indiana University, 1968, pp. 141-60.
Reviews (of the volume):
.1. R.O. Jones, *BHS*, XLVII (1970), 63-4.
.2. Warren T. McCready, *HR*, XXXIX (1971), 214-15.

348 Paxeco, Elza. 'Àcêrca da *Tragicomédia de Dom Duardos*.' In her *Estudos em três línguas*. Lisboa: Pro Domo, 1945, pp. 39-57.
First published in the *Revista da Faculdade de Letras da Universidade de Lisboa*, V (1938), 193-203.

349 Pestana, Sebastião. *Estudos de linguagem*. Porto: Domingos Barreira, [1944].
Ch. i (pp. 7-12) on *Inês Pereira*. Also passing references: pp. 112-13, 120-2, 124, 134-6, 137, 139.

350 —. 'Subsídios para uma edição do *Auto da Alma* de Gil Vicente.' In *Miscelânea de estudos à memória de Cláudio Basto*. Edição organizada por Hermínia Basto. Porto, 1948, pp. 355-66.

351 Providência Costa, João da. 'O problema religioso na obra de Gil Vicente.' In *A evolução e o espírito do teatro em Portugal. 2º ciclo (1ª série) de conferências promovido pelo "Século"*. Lisboa: "O Século", 1947, pp. 83-131.

352 Ramalho, Américo da Costa. 'A *feia acção* de Gil Vicente.' In *Actas do V Colóquio Internacional de Estudos Luso-brasileiros (Coimbra, 1963)*. Vol. IV. Coimbra: Universidade, 1966, pp. 201-6 (2 plates included). Disproves Braamcamp Freire's claim that Gil Vicente was pre-judging Garcia Moniz in a scene of the *Auto da Barca do Inferno*. The essay appeared again, in abridged form, in the *Diário de Notícias* (Lisboa, 27 July 1965). See also following entry.

353 —. *Estudos sobre a época do Renascimento*. Coimbra: Instituto de Alta Cultura, 1969.
Includes: 'Uma alusão vicentina?' (pp. 119-23): from *Colóquio*, 39 (June 1966), 29-30 (in his "Sermão" Gil Vicente possibly alludes to D. Diogo de Sousa). 'A *feia acção* de Gil Vicente' (pp. 124-9). 'Uma bucólica grega em Gil Vicente' (pp. 130-49): from *Humanitas*, Coimbra, XV-XVI (1963-4), 328-47 (on Gil Vicente's adaptation—in *Frágua de Amor*—of Moschus' "Amor fugitivus"). ' "A nossa Júlia modesta" ' (pp. 150-58): on a verse from the *Triunfo do Inverno*. 'Algumas observações sobre o latim de Gil Vicente' (pp. 159-73): from *Humanitas*, XVII-XVIII

(1965-6), 198-210 (Gil Vicente was not as ignorant of Latin as Carolina Michaëlis had assumed). 'Notas' (pp. 174-83).
Reviews:
.1. Hernâni Cidade, *Colóquio*, 60 (October 1970), 76-7.
.2. José V. de Pina Martins, *Euphrosyne*, IV (1970), 343-50.
.3. Domingos Maurício, *Brotéria*, XC (1970), 143.
.4. Gerald M. Moser, *Hispania*, LIII (1970), 318.
.5. A.R., *Brotéria*, XCI (1970), 119-20.
.6. José María Viqueira, *Arbor*, LXXV (1970), 97-102.
.7. Adrien Roig, *Arquivos do Centro Cultural Português*, IV (1972), 785-90.
.8. Edward Glaser, *HR*, XLI (1973), 112-14 [see the author's response to Glaser's review ('Correcções a uma crítica'), also in *HR*, XLI (1973), 713-15].

354   Rangel-Guerrero, Daniel. 'Gil Vicente. *Comédia sobre a divisa da cidade de Coimbra:* una interpretación.' In *Proceedings of the Pacific Northwest Conference on Foreign Languages. Twenty-fifth Annual Meeting (April 19-20, 1974), Eastern Washington State College*. Vol. XXV, Part 1: *Literature and Linguistics*. Ed. Walter C. Kraft. Corvallis: Oregon State University, 1974, pp. 40-4.

354A   —. 'La responsabilidad en la *Comédia de Rubena*.' In *Proceedings of the Pacific Northwest Conference on Foreign Languages (April 17-19, 1975)*, vol. XXVI, Part 1, pp. 154-8.

355   Raposo, Hipólito. 'Anjos e demónios de Gil Vicente.' In his *Amar e servir: história e doutrina*. Porto: Livraria Civilização, 1940, pp. 1-34.

356   Rebello, Luiz Francisco. *O jogo dos homens: ensaios, crónicas e críticas de teatro*. Lisboa: Edições Ática, 1971.
Includes: 'No centenário de Gil Vicente. 1—Dualidade do teatro vicentino', pp. 23-33 (originally a "comunicação lida no Simpósio Vicentino, em 3 de dezembro de 1965"). '2—Actualidade de Gil Vicente', pp. 33-8: from *Seara Nova*, XLIV (1965), 208. See also below, nos 578, 652.

357   Reckert, Stephen. ' "Bajo el signo del latín": cultura literaria de Gil Vicente.' In *Studia hispánica in honorem R. Lapesa*. Vol. III. Madrid: Gredos & Cátedra-Seminario Menéndez Pidal, 1975, pp. 391-403.
Establishes parallels between Johann Geiler von Kaysersberg's sermons and several of Gil Vicente's works, and between the *Speculum morale* of Vincent de Beauvais and Vicente's "Sermão". Concludes that Gil Vicente was more versed in Latin than has been assumed. Revised version included in no. 285A, above.

358   —. 'El verdadero texto de la *Copilaçam* vicentina de 1562.' In *Studia philologica: homenaje ofrecido a Dámaso Alonso por sus amigos y*

discípulos. Vol. III. Madrid: Gredos, 1963, pp. 53-68.

An article of vital importance for textual studies. Since the 1928 facsimile of the 1562 *Copilaçam* is wildly unreliable, it can only be used safely by someone who has Reckert's study before him. Revised version included in no. 285A, above.

Review:
.1. H. Kröll, *ZRP*, LXXX (1964), 583.

358A Révah, Israël Salvator. 'La *comédia* dans l'oeuvre de Gil Vicente.' In his *Études portugaises*. Ed. Charles Amiel. Civilização Portuguesa, III. Paris: Fundação Calouste Gulbenkian/Centro Cultural Português, 1975 [1976], pp. 15-36.
Reproduces no. 599.

359 Ricard, Robert. *'Uno piensa el bayo* . . . Hommage à l'editeur de la *Tragicomedia de Don Duardos.'* In *Studia philologica: homenaje ofrecido a Dámaso Alonso por sus amigos y discípulos*. Vol. III. Madrid: Gredos, 1963, pp. 155-60.
Discusses the use and variants of the proverb "uno piensa el bayo y otro el que lo ensilla" in Hispanic authors. This proverb also occurs in Gil Vicente's *Pranto de Maria Parda.*

360 Rocha, Hildon. 'Gil Vicente em cinco séculos.' In his *Entre lógicos e místicos.* Rio de Janeiro: Livraria São José, 1968, pp. 335-43.

360A Rossi, Giuseppe Carlo. 'Due composizioni bilingui di Gil Vicente: la farsa *Quem tem farelos?* e lo *Auto da Índia.'* In his *Corso di lingua e letteratura portoghese. Anno accademico 1952-1953.* Università degli Studi di Roma. Facoltà di Lettere e Filosofia. Roma: Città Universitaria, La Goliardica, 1953, pp. 50-178.

361 Santos, Víctor. 'Criação do teatro nacional: Gil Vicente.' In his *Sobre a evolução do teatro em Portugal.* Lisboa: Livraria Portugal, 1953, pp. 54-60.

362 Saraiva, António José. 'Gil Vicente, reflexo da crise.' In his *História da cultura em Portugal*. Vol. II. Lisboa: Jornal do Fôro, 1953, pp. 231-368.
On Gil Vicente's ideas and the contrasts reflected in his work.
Review:
.1. I.S. Révah, *BEP*, XIX (1955-6), 221-2.

363 —. *Para a história da cultura em Portugal.* Vol. II. 3rd ed. Lisboa: Europa-América, 1972.
First ed., 1961. Includes: 'Quem era Gil Vicente?' (pp. 295-308): first published in *PRJ* (25 February, 4 and 11 March 1953. See below, nos 515-17); Saraiva rejects the notion that the dramatist and the goldsmith were the same person. 'Gil Vicente e Bertolt Brecht: o papel da ficção na descoberta da realidade' (pp. 309-25): from *Vértice*, XX (1960), 465-75; it has also appeared in *Dionysos*, X, 12 (September 1965), 16-25, and in no. 244, above.

Reviews:
.1. João Mendes, *Brotéria*, LXXIV (1962), 689-95.
.2. Domingos Maurício, *Brotéria*, LXXXVI (1968), 574.
.3. N.J. Lamb, *BHS*, XLVI (1969), 354-6.

364* Saviotti, Gino. *Estética do teatro antigo e moderno*. Lisboa: Tip. Papelaria Fernandes, 1949.
Pp. 47-56 on Gil Vicente.

365 —. 'Gil Vicente e o desenvolvimento do auto sacro (A técnica da representação vicentina).' In his *Filosofia do teatro: tendências estéticas e gôsto representativo das origens à formação do drama moderno*. Lisboa: Inquérito, 1945, pp. 40-9.

366 Sena, Jorge de. *Estudos de história e de cultura (1ª série)*. Vol. I. Lisboa: Revista Ocidente, 1963 [1967].
Includes: 'Gil Vicente e Inês de Castro' (pp. 302-15): discusses *A divisa da cidade de Coimbra* and *A farsa dos almocreves*, where there are references to Inês de Castro. 'Gil Vicente e o Romanceiro' (pp. 315-22): enumerates the ballads utilized by Gil Vicente and claims that they do not occupy a significant place in his dramatic production.
Review:
.1. F. Toriello, *CN*, XXX (1970), 219.

367 Sletsjøe, Leif. 'Las lenguas de Gil Vicente.' In *Actas del XI Congreso Internacional de Lingüística y Filología Románicas (Madrid, 1965)*. Ed. Antonio Quilis. Madrid: CSIC, 1968. Vol. II, pp. 989-1001.

368 Spitzer, Leo. 'La unidad artística del *Auto da Sibila Casandra*.' In his *Sobre antigua poesía española*. Buenos Aires: EUDEBA, 1962, pp. 106-28.
First published, as 'The Artistic Unity of Gil Vicente's *Auto da Sibila Casandra*', in *HR*, XXVII (1959), 56-77.

369 Stegagno Picchio, Luciana. *Ricerche sul teatro portoghese*. Officina Romanica, XIV. Studi e Testi Portoghesi e Brasiliani, IX. Roma: Ateneo, 1969.
Includes: 'Per una tipologia del teatro portoghese' (pp. 11-34): originally published in Portuguese as part of her 'Quatro lições sobre o teatro português,' in *EIP*, XXVIII (1967), 53-67. 'Considerazioni sui testi saiaghesi di Gil Vicente' (pp. 65-82, followed by a 'Nota bibliografica sul saiaghese.' pp. 83-5): first appeared in *Studi di letteratura spagnola*, ed. Carmelo Samonà (Roma: Facoltà di Magistero e Facoltà di Lettere dell'Università di Roma, 1964), pp. 231-41. 'Saiaghese, lingua rustica portoghese, pavano: considerazioni sulle parlate rustiche nel teatro del Cinquecento' (pp. 87-112): first appeared as *Sulle parlate rustiche nel teatro del Cinquecento: saiaghese, lingua rustica portoghese, pavano*

(Venezia: Studi della Fondazione Cini, 1966). 'Diavolo e inferno nel teatro di Gil Vicente' (pp. 115-55): first published in *AION-SR*, I (1959), 31-59. 'Il *Pater Noster* farcito: interpretazione di un passo di Gil Vicente' (pp. 157-71; 'Poscritta,' pp. 169-71): originally published as 'Il *Pater Noster* dell'*Auto do velho da horta*,' in *AION-SR*, III (1961), 191-8. 'Osservazioni sull'uso di alcuni termini nell'antico teatro portoghese' (pp. 313-33): first appeared in *BdF*, XIX (1960), 131-43. 'Per un'edizione critica dei testi di Gil Vicente' (pp. 335-41): published first in Portuguese in *ESPSL*, 457 (4 December 1965), 4. 'Tradizione testuale ed edizioni critiche delle opere di Gil Vicente. Problemi di metodo' (pp. 343-55; 'Poscritta,' pp. 354-55): parts had appeared, in Portuguese, in the *Diário de Notícias* (9 December 1965). 'Questioni gil-vicentine' (pp. 357-71): from *CN*, XIX (1959), 265-74 (see above, no. 293.1). 'Sul teatro neo-latino in Portogallo' (pp. 373-86): from *CN*, XXIV (1964), 289-94 (see above, no. 321.1).

Review:
.1. José Ares Montes, *RFE*, LIV (1971), 182-7.

370   Sten, Holger. 'Gil Vicente et la théorie de l'art dramatique.' In *Études romanes dédiées à Andreas Blinkenberg à l'occasion de son soixante-dixième anniversaire*. Copenhague: Munksgaard, 1963, pp. 209-19.

371   Trigueiros, Luiz Forjaz. 'Dos Paços da Ribeira ao Solar de D. Maria II.' In his *Páteo das comédias: dois anos de crónicas de teatro*. Lisboa: Ática, 1947, pp. 27-34.
Review of a staging of the *Barcas* in the Teatro Nacional by a student company from Coimbra.

372   Trullemans, Ulla M. 'Afinidad temática de la novela picaresca con las cantigas de escarnio y maldecir galaico-portuguesas y algunas farsas de Gil Vicente.' In her *Huellas de la picaresca en Portugal*. Madrid: Ínsula, 1968, pp. 55-70.
Reviews:
.1. R.C. Willis, *BHS*, XLVI (1969), 279.
.2. Alice R. Clemente, *MLN*, LXXXV (1970), 288-9.
.3. Edward Glaser, *HR*, XL (1972), 323-5.

373   Wertheimer, Elaine C. "Honor, Love and Religion in the Theater before Lope de Vega." Dissertation, The City University of New York, 1975. 351 pp.
See *DAI*, XXXV (1974-5), 7927A. Discusses Gil Vicente in Ch. iv (pp. 200-68).

374   Ynduráin, Francisco. 'La dramaturgia de Gil Vicente: ensayo de estima-ción,' In his *De lector a lector*. Madrid: Escelicer, 1973, pp. 25-43.
Originally appeared as two articles: 'La dramaturgia de Gil Vicente:

ensayo de estimación', *Colóquio*, 59 (June 1970), 60-3; and 'La drama-turgia de Gil Vicente: *Don Duardos*,' *CoL*, 2 (June 1971), 14-21.

375 Zamora Vicente, Alonso. 'Una introducción a la *Comédia do viúvo.*'
In *Studia philologica: homenaje ofrecido a Dámaso Alonso por sus amigos y discípulos*. Vol. III. Madrid: Gredos, 1963, pp. 619-34.
The first part of the Introduction to his edition of the play. See above, no. 144.

C. Histories and dictionaries of literature, music, and briefer mentions

376 Alborg, Juan Luis. *Historia de la literatura española*. I: *Edad Media y Renacimiento*. 2nd expanded ed. Madrid: Gredos, 1970, pp. 684-703.

376A Alín, José María. *El cancionero español de tipo tradicional*. Estudios Literarios Sillar, IV. Madrid: Taurus, 1968. 786 pp.
Numerous references to Gil Vicente. Includes also texts of over 50 poems and fragments from his work.

377 Alonso Cortés. Narciso. *Historia de la literatura española*. 6th ed. Valladolid: Librería Santarén, 1951, pp. 125-6.

378 Andrade, Arsénio Sampaio de. *Dicionário histórico e biográfico de artistas e técnicos portugueses (séculos XIV-XX). Sobre a vida e activi-dade, tanto em Portugal como no estrangeiro, de pintores, escultores, ceramistas, gravadores, cinzeladores, arquitectos, caricaturistas, críticos de arte, engenheiros, músicos, contrapontistas, compositores, etc.* . Lisboa, 1959, pp. 90-1.

379 Aubrun, Charles V. *Histoire du théâtre espagnol*. Paris: PUF, 1965, pp. 30-5.
Review:
.1. Bertil Maler, *Ibero-Romanskt*, I (1966), 72-3.

380 Bataillon, Marcel. *Erasmo y España: estudios sobre la historia espiritual del siglo XVI*. Trans. Antonio Alatorre. 2nd ed. México & Buenos Aires: Fondo de Cultura Económica, 1966, pp. 57-8, 612-14, *et passim.*
First ed., in two vols, 1950. Original French ed.: *Erasme et l'Espagne: recherches sur l'histoire spirituelle du XVIe siècle* (Paris: E. Droz, 1937), lix + 903 pp. Originally his thesis for the Université de Paris. Bataillon rejects Erasmus' reputed influence on Gil Vicente.
Reviews:
.1. L. Santullano, *La Nueva Democracia*, 31 (April 1951), 64-72.
.2. Otis H. Green, *HR*, XX (1952), 75-7.
.3. E. Allison Peers, *BHS*, XXIX (1952), 121-2.
.4. Agapito Rey, *Symposium*, VI (1952), 225-9.
.5. H.C. Woodbridge, *Hispania*, XXXV (1952), 126.
.6. María Rosa Lida de Malkiel, *RPhi*, VII (1953-4), 401.

.7. Valeriano Bozal, *CH*, 215 (November 1967), 429-34.
.8. A.M. Garibay K., *Lectura*, 165 (1967), 58-60.
.9. Eugenio Asensio, *Revista de Occidente*, XXI (1968), 302-19.
.10. Miquel Batllori, *AHSI*, XXXVII (1968), 169-71.
.11. Derek W. Lomax, *BHS*, XLV (1968), 82.
.12. F. Márquez Villanueva, *HR*, XXXVI (1968), 264-70.
.13. Elias L. Rivers, *MLN*, LXXXIII (1968), 353.

381 Bell, Aubrey F.G. *Portuguese Literature*. London: Oxford University Press, 1970, pp. 106-31.
Reprint of the 1922 edition. See also his *A literatura portuguesa (história e crítica)*, trans. Agostinho de Campos & J.G. de Barros e Cunha, new rev. ed. (Lisboa: Imprensa Nacional, 1971)—reprint of the 1931 ed. of the Universidade de Coimbra.

382 Blecua, José Manuel. *Historia de la literatura española*. I: *De los orígenes al siglo XVIII*. Zaragoza: Librería General, 1947, pp. 121-4.

383 Boselli, Carlo & Cesco Vian. *Storia della letteratura spagnola dalle origini ad oggi*. 4th rev. ed. Firenze: Valmartina, 1954, pp. 71-2.

384 Branco, João de Freitas. *História da música portuguesa*. Lisboa: Europa-América, 1959, pp. 57-65.
Review:
.1. Pierre Hourcade, *BEP*, XXII (1959-60), 321.

385 Branco, Luís de Freitas. 'A música teatral portuguesa.' In *A evolução e o espírito do teatro em Portugal. 2º ciclo (2ª parte) das conferências promovidas pelo "Século"*. Lisboa: "O Século", 1947, pp. 101-24.

386 Brasil, Reis [José Gomes Bras] . *História da literatura portuguesa*. 3rd ed. Lisboa: Livraria Portugal, 1971, pp. 90-109. (First ed., 1958)

387 Brenan, Gerald. *The Literature of the Spanish People: From Roman Times to the Present Day*. 2nd ed. Cambridge: Cambridge University Press, 1953, pp. 139-45.
(Later reprints; first ed., 1951)
Reviews:
.1. E. Allison Peers, *BHS*, XXVIII (1951), 272-3.
.2. E.M. Wilson, *Clavileño*, 12 (Nov.-Dec. 1951), 76-7.
.3. A. Valtierrra, *Revista Javeriana*, XXXVII (1952), 128.
.4. G.D. Willbern, *Hispania*, XXXV (1952), 371-2.
.5. E.M. Wilson, *MLR*, XLVII (1952), 595-6.
.6. A.A. Parker, *MLR*, LII (1957), 462-3.

388 Brotherton, John. *The "Pastor-Bobo" in the Spanish Theatre before the Time of Lope de Vega*. London: Tamesis, 1975, pp. 17-36, *et passim.*
Reviews:
.1. Victor Dixon, *BHS*, LIV (1977), 150-1.

.2. Charlotte Stern, *RPhi*, XXXI (1977-8), 702-4.

389   Bueno, Francisco da Silveira. *História da literatura luso-brasileira*. 6th updated ed. São Paulo: Saraiva, 1968, pp. 42-4.

389A   Carvalho, José Gonçalo Chorão de. *Os grandes escritores portugueses.* Plano de Educação Popular. 2nd ed. Lisboa: Ministério da Educação Nacional, Direcção-Geral do Ensino Primário, 1965, pp. 41-9. First ed., 1958.

390   Cejador y Frauca, Julio. *Historia de la lengua y literatura castellana*. Vol. I, Part 2. Madrid: Gredos, 1972, pp. 239-42. Facsimile of the 3rd ed. (Madrid: Hernando, 1933).

391   Chandler, Richard E. & Kessel Schwartz. *A New History of Spanish Literature*. Baton Rouge: Louisiana State University Press, 1961, pp. 75-7.

392   Cidade, Hernâni António. *A literatura portuguesa e a expansão ultramarina. As idéias. Os factos. As formas de arte*. I: *Séculos XV e XVI*. 2nd rev. & expanded ed. Coimbra: Arménio Amado, 1963, pp. 79-90. ('O teatro vicentino.' First ed.: Lisboa: Agência Geral das Colónias, 1943)
    Reviews:
    .1. João Maia, *Brotéria,* LXXVII (1963), 488-9.
    .2. P.C. Soromenho, *BMSLP*, XIV (1963), 147-9.
    .3. Giuseppe Carlo Rossi, *Dialoghi*, XIII (1965), 528-30.
    .4. Raymond Cantel, *BEP*, XXVII (1966), 283-5.

393   —. *Lições de cultura e literatura portuguesas*. I. *Séculos XV, XVI e XVII*. 5th rev. & updated ed. Coimbra: Coimbra Editora, 1968, pp. 196-222. ('Aspecto geral do teatro vicentino')

394   —. *Lições de cultura luso-brasileira: épocas e estilos na literatura e nas artes plásticas*. Rio de Janeiro: Livros de Portugal, 1960, pp. 115-25. ('Gil Vicente e seu teatro')
    Reviews:
    .1. João Maia, *Brotéria*, LXXIII (1961), 460-2.
    .2. B.A., *Vértice*, XXII (1962), 327-30.

395   —. *Portugal histórico-cultural*. 2nd rev. & expanded ed. Lisboa: Arcádia, 1968, pp. 93-120. ('Gil Vicente e o comentário das nossas grandezas e servidões')

396   Correia, Fernando da Silva. *V Centenário do nascimento da rainha D. Leonor. 2 de maio de 1958*. São Paulo: Gráfica Biblos, 1958. 59 pp. (Passing references)

397   Costa Pimpão, Álvaro Júlio da. 'As correntes dramáticas na literatura portuguesa do século XVI.' In *A evolução e o espírito do teatro em Portugal. 2º ciclo (1ª série) de conferências promovido pelo "Século"*. Lisboa: "O Século", 1947, pp. 133-68. On Gil Vicente, Jorge Ferreira de Vasconcelos, António Ferreira, Camões.

398 Crawford, James P. Wickersham. *Spanish Drama before Lope de Vega.*
Revised ed. with a Bibliographical Supplement by Warren T. McCready.
Philadelphia: University of Pennsylvania Press, 1967, pp. 33-7, 53-4,
62-7, 101-4.
Reviews:
.1. Anon., *TLS* (10 October 1968), 1162.
.2. Walter Poesse, *Hispanic American Historical Review*, XLVIII
(1968), 548.
.3. Charlotte Stern, *HR*, XXXVI (1968), 360-2.
.4. D.R. Larson, *RPhi*, XXIII (1969-70), 359-61.
.5. Ivy L. McClelland, *Theatre Research/Recherches Théâtrales*,
XI (1971), 59.

First edition (1922):
.6. S. Griswold Morley, *MLN*, XXXVIII (1923), 295-9.
.7. William J. Entwistle, *MLR*, XIX (1924), 248-9.
.8. A.H. Krappe, *Archivum Romanicum*, VIII (1924), 178-80.
.9. Georges Cirot, *BH*, XXVII (1925), 358-61.
.10. W. von Wurzbach, *LGRP*, XLVI (1925), 372-4.

Second edition (1937):
.11. Henry Grattan Doyle, *MLJ*, XXII (1937), 149.
.12. J.T. Reid, *Hispania*, XX (1937), 296.
.13. Aubrey F.G. Bell, *Bulletin of Spanish Studies*, XV (1938),
49-52.
.14. H.C. Heaton, *MLN*, LIII (1938), 461-2.
.15. R.E. House, *HR*, VI (1938), 270-1.
.16. W.K. Jones, *BAbr*, XII (1938), 113-14.
.17. Alexander A. Parker, *MLR*, XXXIII (1938), 465.
.18. Joseph E. Gillet, *RR*, XXX (1939), 80.
.19. A. Kuhn, *ZRP*, LX (1940), 319-20.
.20. Jonas Andries van Praag, *Neophilologus*, XXV (1941), 304-5.
.21. Frida Weber, *Revista de Filología Hispánica*, V (1943), 180-2.

399 Cruz, Maria Antonieta de Lima. *História da música portuguesa.* Lisboa:
Dois Continentes, 1955, pp. 103-20.
('O teatro vicentino precursor da ópera nacional')

400 Cunha, Arlindo Ribeiro da. *A língua e a literatura portuguesa. História
e crítica.* 6th ed. Braga: Edição do autor, 1963, pp. 198-212.

400A Díaz-Plaja, Guillermo & Francisco Monterde. *Historia de la literatura
española. Historia de la literatura mexicana.* 4th ed. México: Editorial
Porrúa, 1965, pp. 127-9.
(First ed., 1955)

401 *Diccionario de literatura española.* Ed. Germán Bleiberg &Julián Marías.

4th rev. & expanded ed. Madrid: Ediciones de la Revista Occidente, 1972, pp. 933-4.
Entry on Gil Vicente by Alonso Zamora.
Review:
.1. Donald Bleznick, *Hispania*, LVII (1974), 195-6.

402 Díez Borque, José María. *Aspectos de la oposición "caballero-pastor" en el primer teatro castellano (Lucas Fernández, Juan del Enzina, Gil Vicente).*Bordeaux: Institut d'Études Ibériques et Ibero-Américaines de l'Université de Bordeaux, 1970. 22 pp.

403 Díez-Echarri, Emiliano & José María Roca Franquesa. *Historia de la literatura española e hispanoamericana.* 2nd ed. Madrid: Aguilar, 1968, pp. 282-4, *et passim.*

404 Di Stefano, Giuseppe. *Sincronia e diacronia nel Romanzero (Un esempio di lettura).* Pisa: Istituto di Letteratura Spagnola e Ispano-Americana, 1967, pp. 91-100.
Examines the survival of the "Romance del rey moro que perdió a Valencia" in the *Auto da Lusitânia.*
Reviews:
.1. Margherita Morreale, *RdL*, XXXV (1969), 217-20.
.2. Colin Smith, *BHS*, XLVIII (1971), 154-6.

405 *Enciclopedia de la cultura española*. Ed. Florentino Pérez-Embid. Vol. V. Madrid: Editora Nacional, 1963, p. 641.
Entry on Gil Vicente by Rafael Morales.

406 Ferreira, Joaquim. *História da literatura portuguesa.* 2nd ed. Porto: Domingos Barreira, 194-?, pp. 204-69.
(First ed., 1939)

407* —. *Sinopse da literatura portuguesa.* Porto: Domingos Barreira, 1967. 140 pp.

408 Figueiredo, Fidelino de. *A épica portuguesa no século XVI.* São Paulo: Faculdade de Filosofia, Ciências e Letras da Universidade de São Paulo, 1950, pp. 117-44.
('O teatro primitivo e os descobrimentos')
Review:
.1. Justino Mendes de Almeida, *Brasília*, V (1950), 684-95.

409 —. *História da literatura clássica. I Época (1502-1580).* 3rd rev. ed. São Paulo: Editora Anchieta, 1946, pp. 55-98.
(First ed.: Lisboa: A.M. Teixeira, 1917)

410 —. *Historia de la literatura portuguesa.* Trans. Marqués de Lozoya. 2nd ed. Barcelona: Labor, 1948, pp. 44-51, 55-7, *et passim.*
(First ed., 1927)

411 —. *História literária de Portugal: séculos XII-XX*. 3rd ed. São Paulo: Editora Nacional, 1966, pp. 111-19.
First ed.: Coimbra: Nobel, 1944. There is also a Spanish version: *Historia literaria de Portugal: siglos XII-XX*. 3 vols. Buenos Aires: Espasa-Calpe, 1948-9.

412 —. *Literatura portuguesa: desenvolvimento histórico das origens à actualidade*. 3rd ed. Rio de Janeiro: Livraria Acadêmica, 1955, pp. 79-84. (First ed.: Rio de Janeiro: A Noite, 1941)

413 Fitzmaurice-Kelly, James. *A New History of Spanish Literature*. New York: Russell& Russell, 1968, pp. 160-3.
Reprint of the 1926 edition.

414 Foster, David William. *Christian Allegory in Early Hispanic Poetry*. Studies in Romance Languages, IV. Lexington: The University Press of Kentucky, 1970, pp. 60-9.
Discusses the *Auto da história de Deus* and, very briefly, the *Auto da sibila Cassandra*.

415 Franzbach, Martin. *Abriss der spanischen und portugiesischen Literaturgeschichte in Tabellen*. Frankfurt am Main: Athenäum Verlag, 1968, pp. 185-7, *et passim.*
    Review:
    .1. Ann L. Mackenzie, *BHS*, XLVII (1970), 68-9.

416 Frèches, Claude-Henri. *La Littérature portugaise*. Paris: PUF, 1970, pp. 47-50.

417 Gallo, Ugo. *Storia della letteratura spagnola*. Milano: Accademia, 1952, pp. 231-4.
(2nd ed., 1958)
    Review:
    .1. Annamaria Gallina, *QIA*, II (1953-4), 376-7.

418 García López, José. *Historia de la literatura española*. 11th ed. New York: Las Américas, 1967, pp. 165-8.

419 Giese, Wilhelm. *Geschichte der spanischen und portugiesischen Literatur*. Bonn: Athenäum, 1949, pp. 86-7, *et passim.*
    Review:
    .1. S. Griswold Morley, *HR*, XIX (1951), 87.

419A Gillet, Joseph E. *"Propalladia" and Other Works of Bartolomé de Torres Naharro*. IV: *Torres Naharro and the Drama of the Renaissance*. Ed. Otis H. Green. Philadelphia: University of Pennsylvania Press, 1961. 645 pp. Numerous references to Gil Vicente throughout.

420 González López, Emilio. *Historia de la literatura española*. I : *Edad Media y Siglo de Oro*. New York: Las Américas, 1962, pp. 210-18.

421   *Grande dicionário de literatura portuguesa e de teoria literária.* Ed.
       João José Cochofel. Lisboa: Iniciativas Editoriais.
       Is being issued in fascicles. Vol. I (1974-1975) includes the following
       entries by Stephen Reckert: 'Almocreves, Farsa dos' (p. 170); 'Barcas,
       Autos das' (pp. 607-24). Revised version of second entry included in
       no. 285A, above.

422   Guerrieri Crocetti, Camillo. *Letteratura spagnola-portoghese.* In vol. II
       of *Storia delle letterature moderne d'Europa e d'America.* Ed. Carlo
       Pellegrini. Milano: Francesco Vallardi, 1959, pp. 226-7.

423   Hess, Rainer. *Das romanische geistliche Schauspiel als profane und
       religiöse Komödie. 15. und 16. Jahrhundert.* München: Wilhelm Fink,
       1965. 198 pp. (Numerous references to Gil Vicente). Revision of his
       doctoral dissertation: "Komische Elemente im geistlichen Schauspiel des
       15. und 16. Jahrhunderts," Freiburg im Breisgau, 1961. There is also a
       Spanish version: *El drama religioso románico como comedia religiosa y
       profana (siglos XV y XVI),* trans. Rafael de la Vega (Madrid: Gredos,
       1976), 333 pp.
       Reviews:
       .1. Winfried Engler, *Zeitschrift für Französische Sprache und Literatur,*
           LXXVI (1966), 381-3.
       .2. M. Nerlich, *RF,* LXXVIII (1966), 582-6.
       .3. José Antonio Míguez, *Arbor,* XCVII (1977), 141-3 [of the Spanish
           version].
       .4. Nigel Griffin, *BHS,* LV (1978), 147-8 [of the Spanish version].

424   *Historia de la literatura española.* I: *Edad Media y Renacimiento.* Ed.
       José María Díez Borque. Madrid: Guadiana, 1975, pp. 690-6.

425   *Historia general de las literaturas hispánicas.* Ed. Guillermo Díaz-Plaja.
       Vol. III. *Renacimiento y barroco.* Barcelona: Barna, 1953, pp. 119-28
       (by Eduardo Juliá Martínez).

426   Hurtado y Jiménez de la Serna, Juan & Ángel González-Palencia. *Historia
       de la literatura española.* 6th ed. Madrid: SAETA, 1949, pp. 324-7, *et
       passim.*

427   Jong, M. de. *Beknopte Geschiedenis der portugese Letterkunde* [A Short
       History of Portuguese Literature]. Amsterdam: L.J. Veen, 1958?,
       pp. 27-41.

428   Le Gentil, Georges. *La Littérature portugaise.* 2nd rev. & enlarged ed.
       Paris: Armand Colin, 1951, pp. 37-44.
       (First ed., 1935)

429   Le Gentil, Pierre. *La Poésie lyrique espagnole et portugaise à la fin du
       Moyen Âge.* I. *Les Thèmes et les genres.* Rennes: Plihon, 1949. 617 pp.

II. *Les Formes*. Rennes: Plihon, 1953. 505 pp.
 Reviews:
 .1. Charles V. Aubrun, *BH*, LI (1949), 429-34 [on vol. I].
 .2. I.S. Révah, *BEP*, XIII (1949), 231-8 [on vol. I].
 .3. Eugenio Asensio, *RFE*, XXXIV (1950), 286-304 [on vol. I].
 .4. J. do Prado Coelho, *RFLUL*, XIV (1950), 215-19 [on vol. I].
 .5. Otis H. Green, *HR*, XIX (1951), 353-7 [on vol. I].
 .6. D.W. McPheeters, *RR*, XLII (1951), 284-7 [on vol. I].
 .7. María Rosa Lida de Malkiel, *Speculum*, XXVI (1951), 174-9
  and XXVIII (1953), 905-8.
 .8. Otis H. Green, *RPhi*, VIII (1954-5), 151-3 [on vol. II].
 .9. Dorothy Clotelle Clarke, *HR*, XXIII (1955), 61-8 [on vol. II].

429A Lida de Malkiel, María Rosa. 'La visión de trasmundo en las literaturas hispánicas.' Appended (pp. 371-449) to Howard Rollin Patch, *El otro mundo en la literatura medieval*, trans. Jorge Hernández Campos (México & Buenos Aires: Fondo de Cultura Económica, 1956).
 For Gil Vicente, see pp. 439-41 *et passim*.

429B Lihani, John. *El lenguaje de Lucas Fernández: estudio del dialecto sayagués*. Publicaciones del Instituto Caro y Cuervo, XXXI. Bogotá: Instituto Caro y Cuervo, 1973, pp. 21-7, 29-30, 32-5, 49-50, *et passim*.
 Review:
 .1. Steven Hess, *BCom*, XXVI (1974), 84-5.

430 López Morales, Humberto. 'Elementos leoneses en la lengua del teatro pastoril de los siglos XV y XVI.' In *Actas del Segundo Congreso Internacional de Hispanistas celebrado en Nijmegen del 20 al 25 de agosto de 1965*. Ed. Jaime Sánchez-Romeralo & Norbert Poulussen. Nijmegen: Instituto Español de la Universidad de Nimega, 1967, pp. 411-19.

431 —. *Tradición y creación en los orígenes del teatro castellano*. Madrid: Ediciones Alcalá, 1968, pp. 121-4, 134-40, 145-6, *et passim*.
 Reviews:
 .1. Edwin J. Webber, *MPhi*, LXVII (1969-70), 373-6.
 .2. Michael J. Ruggerio, *RPhi*, XXIV (1970-1), 541-5.

432 Mancini Giancarlo, Guido. *Storia della letteratura spagnola*. Milano: Feltrinelli, 1961, pp. 227-9.

433 Martínez Torner, Eduardo. *Lírica hispánica: relaciones entre lo popular y lo culto*. Madrid: Castalia, 1966. 459 pp. An expanded version of 'Índice de analogías entre la lírica española antigua y la moderna,' *Symposium*, I, 1 (November 1946), 12-33; I, 2 (May 1947), 4-35; I, 3 (November 1947), 84-107; II (1948), 84-105, 221-41; III (1949), 282-320; V (1950), 141-80.
 (Numerous references to Gil Vicente)

Reviews:
.1. C.C. Smith, *BHS*, XLV (1968), 223-4.
.2. Roberto Paoli, *RPhi*, XXV (1971-2), 247-52.

434 Martins, Mário. *Teatro quinhentista nas naus da Índia*. Lisboa: Edições "Brotéria", 1973, pp. 9-11, 52-5, *et passim*.
Review:
.1. Lucília Gonçalves Pires, *CoL*, 16 (November 1973), 89.

434A *McGraw-Hill Encyclopedia of World Drama: An International Reference Work in Four Volumes*. New York: McGraw-Hill, 1972.
Entry on Gil Vicente (no mention of contributor): IV, pp. 356-9.

434B Menéndez Pidal, Ramón. *Romancero hispánico (hispano-portugués, americano y sefardí): Teoría e historia*. II. Obras Completas de R. Menéndez Pidal, X. 2nd ed. Madrid: Espasa-Calpe, 1968, pp. 103-6 ('El romance en los comienzos del teatro. Época de Gil Vicente'), 209-10, 216, 326, 372-3. First ed., 1953.
Reviews:
.1. I.S. Révah, *BEP*, XVII (1953), 265-70.
.2. S. Griswold Morley, *RPhi*, XI (1957-8), 311-17.

435 Moisés, Massaud. *A literatura portuguêsa*. 3rd rev. ed. São Paulo: Cultrix, 1965, pp. 51-61.
Review:
.1. João Décio, *Alfa*, 7-8 (1965), 233-5.

436 Montolíu y de Togores, Manuel de. *Manual de historia de la literatura castellana*. 5th ed. Barcelona: Editorial Cervantes, 1947, pp. 618-21. (First ed., 1929)

437 Oliveira, José Osório de. *La Littérature portugaise*. Trans. Jean Bayle. Lisbonne: Éditions SNI, n.d., pp. 16-19.

438 Orfão, José Joaquim de Matos & Pedro Homem de Mello. *História da literatura portuguesa. Esquemas para o ensino técnico profissional*. Porto: Educação Nacional, 1968?, pp. 27-34.

439 *Oxford Companion to the Theatre*. Ed. Phyllis Hartnoll. 3rd ed. London: Oxford University Press, 1967.
Entry on the Portuguese theater by A.D. Deyermond (pp. 753-7).

440 Parker, Jack Horace. *Breve historia del teatro español*. Manuales Studium, VI. México: Ediciones de Andrea, 1957, pp. 17-18.

441 Pedro, António. *O teatro e a sua verdade. Conferência realizada no Instituto Superior Técnico de Lisboa em 31 de março de 1950*. Lisboa: Confluência, [1950], pp. 20-3.

442 *The Penguin Companion to Literature:* II. *European*. Ed. A.K. Thorlby.

Harmondsworth: Penguin Books, 1969.
Entry on Gil Vicente by A.R. Milburn, pp. 800-2.

443 Pereira Dias, João. 'Dos momos e arremedilhos ao cenário sintético (encenação).' In *A evolução e o espírito do teatro em Portugal. 2º ciclo (1ª série) de conferências promovido pelo "Século"*. Lisboa: "O Século", 1947, pp. 21-49.

444 Pereira Tavares, José. *Como se devem ler os clássicos*. Lisboa: Livraria Sá da Costa, 1941, pp. 54-7 ('A linguagem vicentina'), 145-55.

445 Piccolo, Francesco. *Storia della letteratura portoghese*. Milano: Nuova Accademia, 1961, pp. 71-89.
   Review:
   .1. P. Lidmilová, *PP*, VI (1963), 441-2.

446 Pinto, Dinah Sonia Renault. *Pequena história da literatura portuguêsa*. Rio de Janeiro: Melso, 1964, pp. 68-76.

447 Porrata, Francisco E. *Incorporación del romancero a la temática de la comedia española*. Madrid: Plaza Mayor, 1973, pp. 36-8.
   Deals briefly with Gil Vicente's utilization of the ballad at the end of *Dom Duardos*.
   Reviews:
   .1. Gregorio Torres Nebrera, *ELit*, 526 (15 October 1973), 1498-1500.
   .2. Janet W. Díaz, *Hispanófila*, 58 (September 1976), 88-9.

448 Ramos, Feliciano. *História da literatura portuguesa desde o século XII aos meados do século XX*. 4th rev. & expanded ed. Braga: Livraria Cruz, 1960, pp. 219-56.
   ('Gil Vicente e o teatro do Renascimento')
   Review:
   .1. M.B.F., *Ocidente*, LIV (1958), 97-8.

448A *The Reader's Encyclopedia of World Drama*. Ed. John Gassner & Edward Quinn. New York: Thomas Y. Crowell, 1969.
   Entry on Gil Vicente by Joel Pontes, pp. 897-8; also pp. 675-6 (Pontes) and 795-6 (Wardropper).

449 Rebello, Luiz Francisco. *História do teatro português*. 2nd ed. Lisboa: Europa-América, 1972, pp. 28-35.
   ('Gil Vicente ou a maioridade')
   First ed., 1968. See also: Rebello, *El teatro portugués*, trans. Jofre Barroso (Buenos Aires: Centro Editor de América Latina, 1968), 103 pp.
   Reviews:
   .1. N.J. Lamb, *BHS*, XLVI (1969), 179-80.
   .2. Michael Ricciardelli, *BAbr*, XLIII (1969), 587-8.

450 Reckert, Stephen. *Lyra Minima: Structure and Symbol in Iberian*

Traditional Verse [London: King's College,] 1970, pp. 12, 14-15, 23-4, 26, 33, 36-7, 41-2, 44, 46.
Review:
.1. J.G. Cummins, *BHS*, XLVIII (1971), 350-1.

451 Révah, I.S. 'Gil Vicente.' In *Dicionário de literatura portuguesa, brasileira, galega. Estilística literária.* Ed. Jacinto do Prado Coelho. 3rd ed. Porto: Figueirinhas, 1973. Vol. IV, pp. 1164-9.
First ed., 1960. Includes short entries on individual works, too. Révah's article includes his dating of Gil Vicente's plays. It has also appeared in *BGPL*, 2 (May 1965), 29-41.
Reviews:
.1. Luciana Stegagno Picchio, *CN*, XVIII (1958), 293-7 [on the early fascicles].
.2. Raymond Cantel, *BH*, LXIV (1962), 346-7.

452 Río, Ángel del. *Historia de la literatura española. I: Desde los orígenes hasta 1700.* Rev. ed. New York: Holt, Rinehart & Winston, 1963, pp. 213-15.

453 Rossi, Giuseppe Carlo. *Geschichte der portugiesischen Literatur.* Trans. Erika Rossi-Rupprecht. Tübingen: Max Niemeyer, 1964, pp. 58-71.
Translation of the following entry in rev. and updated form.
Reviews:
.1. Klaus Rühl, *RJ*, XVI (1965), 374-84.
.2. Georg Schurhammer, *AHSI*, XXXV (1966), 258-9.
.3. A.E. Beau, *ASNSL*, CCIV (1967), 153-60.
.4. Herbert Koch, *Deutsche Literaturzeitung*, LXXXI (1967), cols 898-900.
.5. Wolfgang Riethmüller, *Bücherei und Bildung*, XIX (1967), 744.
.6. Edward Glaser, *HR*, XXXVI (1968), 294-9.
.7. B.N. Teensma, *Neophilologus*, LII (1968), 93.
.8. Arion Ehrhardt, *ZRP*, LXXXVII (1971), 175-81.

454 —. *Storia della letteratura portoghese.* Firenze: Sansoni, 1953, pp. 46-56.
Reviews:
.1. J.M. Azáceta, *RFE*, XXXVII (1953), 332-3.
.2. J. do Prado Coelho, *BdF*, XIV (1953), 175-81.
.3. Guido Battelli, *QIA*, II (1953-4), 449-51.
.4. B. Crippa, *Humanitas* (Brescia), IX (1954), 614-15.
.5. María Rosa Lida de Malkiel, *RPhi*, VIII (1954-5), 153-5.
.6. Luigi Panarese, *Rivista di Letterature Moderne e Comparate*, VIII (1955), 63-6.
.7. António Zagalo, *RF*, LXVII (1955), 220-1.
.8. A. Rüegg, *ZRP*, LXXII (1956), 161-2.

455   Ruiz Ramón, Francisco. *Historia del teatro español*. I: *Desde sus orígenes hasta 1900*. 2nd ed. Madrid: Alianza Editorial, 1971, pp. 85-95. (First ed., 1967)
      Reviews:
      .1. F.A.P., *El Libro Español*, X (1967), 725.
      .2. Francisco Aguilar Piñal, *RdL*, XXXI (1967), 201-5.
      .3. J.E. Aragonés, *ELit*, 373 (1 July 1967), 24-5.
      .4. Enrique Rull, *Segismundo*, III (1967), 400-1.
      .5. Amos Segala, *Il Dramma*, XLV (1969), 11.
      .6. Jack H. Parker, *HR*, XXXVIII (1970), 328-9.

456   Sainz de Robles, Federico Carlos. *El teatro español: historia y antología (desde el siglo XIV al XIX)*. I: *Desde Rodrigo de Cota hasta Cervantes*. Madrid: Aguilar, 1942, pp. 523-99. Pp. 523-33 on Gil Vicente. Pp. 535-99: the text of the *Tragicomedia de Don Duardos* (based on Dámaso Alonso's ed.).
      Review:
      .1. Erich von Richthofen, *ZRP*, LXVI (1950), 222-7.

457   ——. *Ensayo de un diccionario de la literatura*. II. *Escritores españoles e hispanoamericanos*. 3rd ed. Madrid: Aguilar, 1964, pp. 1247-50.

458   Saraiva, António José. *A Inquisição portuguesa*. 3rd rev. ed. Lisboa: Europa-América, 1964, pp. 98-100, *et passim*.

459   ——. *Breve historia de la literatura portuguesa*. Trans. J.A.L. Madrid: Istmo, 1971, pp. 65-76.
      Translation of the 9th ed. of the following entry.

460   ——. *História da literatura portuguesa*. 10th ed. Lisboa: Europa-América, 1970, pp. 57-68.
      1st ed., 1949.

461   Saraiva, António José & Óscar Lopes. *História da literatura portuguesa*. 4th rev. ed. Porto: Porto Editora & Lisboa: Fluminense, [1964], pp. 175-212.
      Later editions also. First ed., 1954.
      Reviews:
      .1. I.S. Révah, *BEP*, XVIII (1954), 201-2, and XX (1957), 272.
      .2. João Mendes, *Brotéria*, LXII (1956), 205-10.
      .3. Gerald M. Moser, *BAbr*, XXXII (1958), 211-12.
      .4. João Maia, *Brotéria*, LXXXIV (1967), 644-6.

462   Shergold, N.D. *A History of the Spanish Stage from Medieval Times until the End of the Seventeenth Century*. Oxford: Clarendon Press, 1967, pp. 40-1, 133-6, 167-8, *et passim*.
      Reviews:
      .1. Anon., *TLS* (19 October 1967), 986.

.2. Gabriel Jackson, *American Historical Review*, LXXIII (1967), 501.
.3. Anon., *Choice*, IV (1967-8), 1131.
.4. Joseph A. Byrnes, *Seventeenth-Century News*, XXVI (1968), 16.
.5. C.A. Jones, *MLR*, LXIV (1969), 685-6.
.6. Alexander A. Parker, *BHS*, XLVI (1969), 57-60.

463   Simões, João Gaspar. *História da poesia portuguesa das origens aos nossos dias, acompanhada de uma antologia.* Vol. I. Lisboa: Empresa Nacional de Publicidade, 1955, pp. 185-93, 249.
Includes three lyrics (p. 249).

464   —. *Itinerário histórico da poesia portuguesa de 1189 a 1964.* Lisboa: Arcádia, 1964, pp. 57-9, *et passim.*

465   Stegagno Picchio, Luciana. 'Gil Vicente.' In the *Enciclopedia dello spettacolo.* Vol. IX. Roma: Le Maschere, 1962, cols 1636-41.

466   —. *História do teatro português.* Trans. Manuel de Lucena. Lisboa: Portugália, 1969, pp. 39-86.
Translation of the following entry, rev. by the author.
    Review:
    .1. Elêusis M. Camocardi, *Revista de Letras*, XII (1969), 239-44.

467   —. *Storia del teatro portoghese.* Roma: Ateneo, 1964, pp. 19-52.
    Reviews:
    .1. Guido Burgada, *EIP*, XXIII (1964), 262-6.
    .2. Claude-Henri Frèches & Paul Teyssier, *BEP*, XXV (1964), 270-3.
    .3. Aldo Menichetti, *CN*, XXIV (1964), 304.
    .4. Rainer Hess, *RF*, LXXVII (1965), 216-18.
    .5. Wilson Martins, *Hispania*, XLVIII (1965), 943.
    .6. Jean-Michel Massa, *RHTh*, XVIII (1966), 238-40.

467A   Stern, Charlotte. "Studies on the *sayagués* in the Early Spanish Drama." Dissertation, University of Pennsylvania, 1960. 404 pp.
See *DA*, XXI (1960-1), 1195.

468   Ticknor, George. *History of Spanish Literature.* New York: Gordian Press, 1965. Vol. I, pp. 297-306.
Reprint of the 6th ed. (Boston: Houghton Mifflin, 1891).
First ed.: New York: Harper & Bros, 1849.

468A   Torri, Julio. *La literatura española.* Breviarios del Fondo de Cultura Económica, LVI. México: Fondo de Cultura Económica, 1969, pp. 170-4 *et passim.* Reprint of the first ed., 1952.

469   Trend, John Brande. *Lorca and the Spanish Poetic Tradition.* Oxford: Blackwell, 1956, pp. 161-6.

470   *Two Spanish Verse Chapbooks: "Romance de Amadís" (c. 1515-19), "Juyzio hallado y trobado" (c. 1510).* Ed. F.J. Norton & E.M. Wilson.

Cambridge: Cambridge University Press, 1969. x + 94 pp.
Facsimile edition with bibliographical and textual studies. There may be a link between the "Romance de Amadís" and Gil Vicente's *Amadis de Gaula* (see p. 34).
Reviews:
  .1. Bernard Gicovate, *Hispania*, LIII (1970), 147-8.
  .2. Keith Whinnom, *BHS*, XLVII (1970), 150-3.
  .3. Dorothy Clotelle Clarke, *MPhi*, LXVIII (1970-1), 378-80.
  .4. Charlotte Stern, *RPhi*, XXIV (1970-1), 221-4.
  .5. Ruth House Webber, *HR*, XL (1972), 92-4.

471   Valbuena Prat, Ángel. *Historia de la literatura española*. 8th ed. Barcelona: Gustavo Gili, 1968. Vol. I, pp. 452-66.
(First ed., 1937)

472   —. *Historia del teatro español*. Barcelona: Noguer, 1956, pp. 33-9.
Reviews:
  .1. J.L. Cano, *Arbor,* XXXV (1956), 531-2.
  .2. M. Muñoz Cortés, *Clavileño*, 8 (1957), 70-4.
  .3. Raymond R. MacCurdy, *Symposium*, XII (1958), 206-11.
  .4. E. González López, *RHM*, XXV (1959), 241-2.
  .5. Ramón Rozzell, *NRFH*, XIII (1959), 376-80.

473   —. *Literatura dramática española*. 2nd ed. Barcelona: Labor, 1950, pp. 51-66.
Reprint of the 1930 ed.
Reviews:
  .1. Joaquín de Entrambasaguas, *Revista de la Biblioteca, Archivo y Museo del Ayuntamiento de Madrid*, VIII (1931), 212-14.
  .2. Willis Knapp Jones, *BAbr*, V (1931), 264.
  .3. José F. Montesinos, *RFE*, XVIII (1931), 175-80.

474   Valverde, José María. *Breve historia de la literatura española*. Madrid: Guadarrama, 1969, pp. 60-2.

475*   Vian, Cesco. *Storia della letteratura portoghese*. Milano: Fabbri, 1969. 160 pp.

476   Wardropper, Bruce W. *Introducción al teatro religioso del Siglo de Oro: evolución del auto sacramental antes de Calderón*. Salamanca: Anaya, 1967, pp. 172-6.
A slightly rev. and updated version of the first ed. (Madrid: Revista de Occidente, 1953).
Reviews:
  .1.   José Caso González, *Archivum*, III (1953), 443-7.
  *.2.   Juan Emilio Aragonés, *Correo Literario* (15 March 1954).
  .3.   Marcel Bataillon, *BH*, LVI (1954), 431-4.

.4. Courtney Bruerton, *NRFH*, VIII (1954), 328-30.
*.5. Melchor Fernández Almagro, *La Vanguardia* (13 January 1954).
.6. R. de G., *Ínsula*, 100-1 (30 April 1954), 10.
.7. Jerónimo Mallo, *Hispania*, XXXVII (1954), 384-5.
.8. José Montero Padilla, *RdL*, V (1954), 416-18.
.9. Salvador Dinamarca, *RHM*, XXI (1955), 346-7.
.10. H. Lausberg, *ASNSL*, CXCII (1955), 248.
.11. José Montero Padilla, *RFE*, XXXIX (1955), 365-8.
.12. Alexander A. Parker, *BHS*, XXXII (1955), 49-51.
.13. Beatrice Patt, *HR*, XXIII (1955), 68-73.
.14. Edward Sarmiento, *MLR*, L (1955), 223-4.

477 Wilson, Edward M. & Duncan Moir. *A Literary History of Spain: The Golden Age, Drama (1492-1700)*. Ed. R.O. Jones. London: Ernest Benn & New York: Barnes & Noble, 1971, pp. 8-13.
There is also a Spanish version: *Historia de la literatura española. Siglo de Oro: teatro* (Barcelona: Ariel, 1974), 265 pp.
Reviews:
.1. Charles V. Aubrun, *BHS*, L(1973), 171-3.
.2. Elias L. Rivers, *MLN*, LXXXVIII (1973), 507.
.3. José R. Cortina, *MLJ*, LVIII (1974), 80-1.
.4. Charlotte Stern, *RPhi*, XXVIII (1974-5), 139-41.

478 Wilson, Margaret. *Spanish Drama of the Golden Age*. Oxford: Pergamon Press, 1969, pp. 12-13, *et passim.*
Reviews:
.1. Anon., *Modern Languages*, L (1969), 175.
.2. G. St Andrews, *Canadian Modern Language Review*, XXVI (1969), 79.
.3. Elias L. Rivers, *MLN*, LXXXV (1970), 302.
.4. Daniel Rogers, *BHS*, XLVII (1970), 157-9.
.5. C.A. Jones, *MLR*, LXVII (1972), 195-6.

D. Articles in journals

i. General

General

479 Anon. 'V centenário de Gil Vicente.' *Ocidente*, LXX (1966), 15-17.

480* Boto, António. 'Gil Vicente (soneto inédito).' *PRJ* (16 December 1953).

481 Cafèzeiro, Edwaldo. 'Gil Vicente, hoje.' *Dionysos*, X, 12 (September 1965), 40-9.

482 Castelo-Branco, Fernando. 'Simpósio vicentino.' *Panorama*, 17 (1966), 15-20.
Describes the Gil Vicente Symposium which took place in Lisbon in 1965.

483 Dias, Jaime Lopes. 'No V centenário de Gil Vicente.' *Estudos de Castelo Branco*, 18 (1965), 9-25.

484 Ferreira, David Mourão. 'Evocação vicentina.' *Humboldt*, VI (1966), 56-8.

485 Freire, Pascual F.M. 'A personalidade de Gil Vicente.' Trans. Catharina R. Barbosa. *BGPL*, 4 (January 1966), 3-5.

486 Gil Álvarez, Felipe. 'Gil Vicente.' *Haz*, 18 (January-February 1945), 95-8.

487 Gomes, F. Casado. 'Aspectos da obra vicentina.' *BGPL*, 4 (January 1966), 10-27.

488* Granada, Novais. 'Mestre Gil imortal.' *Correio do Ribatejo* (21 August 1965).

489 Lapa, Manuel Rodrigues. 'Ainda e sempre o nosso Mestre Gil.' *Vértice*, XXV (1965), 699-714.

490 Malpique, Cruz. 'Gil Vicente num relámpago.' *GilV*, XVI (1965), 101-5, 145-50.

491 Martins, Mário. 'Gil Vicente.' *Brotéria*, LXXXI (1965), 13-28.

492 Mendes, João. 'Comemoração de Gil Vicente.' *Brotéria*, LXXXI (1965), 111-20.

493 Pinto, Álvaro. 'O culto de Gil Vicente.' *Ocidente*, XLV (1953), 39.

494 Rebello, Luiz Francisco. 'El centenario de Gil Vicente.' *Primer Acto*, 73 (1966), 64-5.
See also following entry.

495 —. 'The Anniversary of Gil Vicente.' *World Theatre*, XIV (1965), 618-20.

496 [Saviotti, Gino]. 'Gil Vicente.' *Livros de Portugal*, 80 (1965), 6-18.

497 Schell, Hermann Ferdinand. 'Gil Vicente.' *Atlântico*, Nova Série, no. 3 (1947), 20-1.
A poem in German, addressed to Gil Vicente. It is followed (pp. 22-3) by Augusto Pinto's free translation into Portuguese.

498 Sena, Jorge de. 'Sobre Gil Vicente. A propósito de um centenário hipotético.' *TeM*, 33 (December 1965), 1136-40.
Also published, as 'Um centenário hipotético', in *ESPSL*, 457 (4 December 1965), 5.

499 Silva, Rui Rosas da & J.B. Mota Amaral. 'Gil Vicente, portuguesíssimo e europeu. Entrevista com o Prof. Claude-Henri Frèches.' *Rumo*, 107 (January 1966), 56-61.

499A Spina, Segismundo. 'Gil Vicente no V Colóquio.' *ESPSL*, 457 (4 December 1965), 3.

500   Zapata Acosta, R. 'Vida y presencia de Gil Vicente.' *Letras*, XXI-XXII (1973-4), 25-37.

Gil Vicente, the Man

501   Brito, Luís Filipe Aviz de. 'Contributo dos notários e guardas-mores para a identificação de Mestre Gil Vicente.' *GilV*, XVI (1965), 69-73.

502*   Campos, António Alves de. 'Gil Vicente cita (e conheceu) Torrozelo.' *Suplemento de "Novidades"*, 58 (5 April 1965).

503   Gambetta, Agostinho Ferreira. 'Gil Vicente moedeiro.' *Nummus*, VII (1962), 3-36.

504   Gomes, Armando Sousa. 'Tentativa de identificação de Gil Vicente.' *O Instituto*, XCVII (1940), 433-61.
       He claims that Gil Vicente went through a series of trades (weaver, tailor, painter, goldsmith) before becoming a poet, and that he was trained in theology but later gave up an ecclesiastical career. See also above, no. 251.

505*   Gonçalves, António Manuel. 'Gil Vicente, ourives.' *ComP* (22 June 1965).

506   Matos Sequeira, Gustavo de. 'Será Gil Vicente-poeta o Gil Vicente-ourives?' *Autores*, 10 (1960), 13.

507   Oliveira, Joaquim de. 'O Gil Vicente-poeta é o Gil Vicente-ourives.' *Autores*, 11 (1961), 19-20.

508*   Peixoto, Armindo. 'Onde nasceu Gil Vicente. Uma testemunha que o Sr. Dr. Aurélio Proença não ouviu.' *NGui* (12 May 1940).
       Reply to no. 510, below.

509*   —. 'Para que todos saibam—Onde nasceu Gil Vicente.' *NGui* (7 April 1940).

510*   Proença, Aurélio. 'Para que todos saibam. Onde nasceu Gil Vicente.' *NGui* (21 April 1940).
       See above, no. 508.

511   Rego, Diogo dos Santos. 'Gil Vicente, lavrador da Beira?' *Boletim da Casa Regional da Beira-Douro*, XIV (1965), 98-102, 183-5, 196-202.

512   Rego, Rogério de Figueiroa. 'A família de Gil Vicente. Novos documentos.' *Arquivo Histórico de Portugal*, I (1961), 311-36.

513   São Payo, Marquês de. 'No V centenário de Gil Vicente. Subsídios para a árvore genealógica da sua descendência.' *Armas e Troféus*, VI (1965), 115-36.

514*   Saraiva, António José. 'Ele [Gil Vicente] e nós.' *ComP* (8 June 1965).

515*   —. 'Gil Vicente *clerc*.' *PRJ* (11 March 1953).

516*   —. 'Quem era Gil Vicente?' *PRJ* (25 February 1953).

517*   —. 'Um ourives e um poeta palaciano.' *PRJ* (4 March 1953).

The Historical and Cultural Milieu

518   Anon. 'Gil Vicente e o seu tempo: tábua sincrónica.' *Vértice*, XXV (1965), 861-77.

519   Carvalho, A. Saraiva de. 'Diálogo com Gil Vicente. O poeta e a história.' *GilV*, XV (1964), 49-54, 75-81, 97-101, 147-58, 169-80.

520*   Castro, Armando de. 'A estrutura económico-social quinhentista reflectida na obra de Gil Vicente.' *ComP* (8 June 1965).

521   —. 'Os principais factores económicos que plasmaram a sociedade da época de Gil Vicente.' *Vértice*, XXV (1965), 677-98.

522   Cidade, Hernâni. 'Gil Vicente: a época, o homem e o poeta.' *Revista de Guimarães*, LXXV (1965), 174-91.

523   Martins Fernandes, M. 'Gil Vicente en el torbellino del siglo XVI.' *El Pensamiento Navarro*, 13 (1965), 9-12.

524   Moseley, William W. ' "O Rei do Mar": Portugal, the Sea, and Gil Vicente.' *L-BR*, XI (1974), 98-104.

525   Nunes, Eduardo. 'A dimensão histórica na obra de Gil Vicente.' *Brotéria*, LXXXII (1966), 50-62.
Gil Vicente opts for myth and comedy rather than history.

526*   Oliveira, Barradas de. 'Gil Vicente e a sociedade.' *Jornal do Ribatejo* (29 July 1965).

527   Toledo, Dionísio de Oliveira. 'A época de Gil Vicente.' *BGPL*, 4 (January 1966), 97-106.

Gil Vicente and Portuguese Drama

528   Adams, Mildred. 'Gil Vicente, Pioneer Playwright.' *Theatre Arts*, XXVI (1942), 275-8.

529   Anon. 'Gil Vicente o primeiro revisteiro português.' *Autores*, 9 (1960), 16-18.

530   Cidade, Hernâni. 'Gil Vicente: repercussão no teatro de Camões.' *Dionysos*, X, 12 (September 1965), 29-39.
Compares the *Tragicomédia de Dom Duardos* with Camões' *Auto de Filodemo*, both of which are protests against the "desigualdade dos estados".

531   Ferreira, Ernesto. 'Reminiscências do teatro vicentino nos Açôres.' *Açoreana*, II (1940), 152-60.

532*   Lemos, Pedro de. 'Gil Vicente, criador da tradicional revista portuguesa.'
       ComP (8 June 1965).

533   Martins, Mário. 'O teatro de Gil Vicente na época de D. Manuel I.'
       Panorama, 32 (1969), 21-6.

534   Miguel, António Dias. 'Entremezes e representações na procissão do
       Corpo de Deus no reinado de D. Manuel (1509-1514).' *Colóquio*, 43
       (April 1967), 65-7.

535   Révah, I.S. 'Gil Vicente a-t-il été le fondateur du théâtre portugais?'
       BHTP, I (1950), 153-85.
       The answer is "yes" so far as his religious pieces are concerned. His
       farces, however, were not created *ex nihilo*.

536   Ribeiro, Mário de Sampayo.'A rainha Dona Leonor de Lancastre e os
       alvores do teatro português.' *Ocidente*, LVI (1959), 69-82.

537   Sletsjøe, Leif. 'O teatro vicentino: uma criação *ex nihilo?*' *Ocidente*,
       LXXXII (1972), 241-7.
       He answers negatively, agreeing with A.J. Saraiva's position that Gil
       Vicente was working within a tradition.

538   Teixeira, António Braz. 'Possibilidade e realidade do teatro português.'
       Espiral, II (1965), 49-53.
       Enumerates Gil Vicente's contributions to Portuguese theater and sur-
       veys subsequent highlights of it.

539   Zeitlin, Marion. 'Gil Vicente e o teatro português.' *Modern Language
       Forum*, XXIX (1944), 85-7.

Gil Vicente and Peninsular Drama

540   Anon. 'A estréia de Gil Vicente.' *Autores*, 20 (1963), 9.

541   Hart, Thomas R. 'The Early Court Theater in Portugal and Valencia:
       Gil Vicente, Luis Milán, Juan Fernández de Heredia.' *MLN*, LXXXVII
       (1972), 307-15.

542   Lima, Fernando de Castro Pires de. 'Influência de Gil Vicente em *Os
       interesses criados* de Jacinto Benavente.'*Revista de Dialectología y
       Tradiciones Populares*, XXVI (1970), 303-13.

543   —. 'Jacinto Benavente actualizou Mestre Gil.' *Tempo Presente*, 13
       (May 1960), 45-56.
       Influence of the *Barca do Inferno* on *Los intereses creados*.

544   Parker, Jack Horace. 'Gil Vicente: A Study in Peninsular Drama.'
       Hispania, XXXVI (1953), 21-5.

545   Sletsjøe, Leif. 'L'Évolution du théâtre dans la Péninsule Ibérique et
       l'oeuvre dramatique de Gil Vicente.'*Revue Romane*, VIII (1973), 272-85.

546   Weber de Kurlat, Frida. 'Relaciones literarias: *La Celestina*, Diego Sánchez de Badajoz y Gil Vicente.' *Philological Quarterly*, LI (1972), 105-22.
La Celestina served as source to both dramatists in matters of magic.

547   Young, Richard A. 'Gil Vicente's Castilian *Début.*' *Segismundo*, 15-16 (1972), 25-50.

Gil Vicente and Extrapeninsular Drama

548   Janeiro, Armando Martins. 'Teatro clássico japonês e teatro ocidental, particularmente o vicentino.' *Colóquio*, 43 (April 1967), 44-7.
See also above, nos 257, 326.

549   Livermore, Ann. 'Gil Vicente and Shakespeare.' *Book Handbook*, II (1951), 1-12.
Also: 'Gil Vicente e Shakespeare.' *RFLUL*, XVII (1951), 140-9. Suggests that Shakespeare may have read Gil Vicente, and draws parallels between the *Triunfo do Inverno* and *The Tempest*. See also above, no. 330.

Gil Vicente and the Theater

550   Deniz-Jacinto. 'O actor numa encenação de Gil Vicente.' *Vértice*, XXV (1965), 799-805.

551   'Inquérito sobre Gil Vicente.' *Vértice*, XXV (1965), 841-57.
Eight personalities, associated with the theater in various capacities, answer a questionnaire on Gil Vicente.

552   Jesus, Eduíno de. 'A dificuldade e a alegria de representar Gil Vicente. Entrevista com o actor-encenador Pedro Lemos.' *Rumo*, 107 (January 1966), 50-6.

553   —. 'Algumas representações do teatro de Gil Vicente no centenário do seu nascimento.' *Rumo*, 107 (January 1966), 65-7.

554   Pedro, António. 'Como seriam postas em cena as peças de Gil Vicente?' *Colóquio*, 36 (December 1965), 49-50.

555   Ribeiro, António Lopes. 'Teatro português: Gil Vicente representado agora.' *Atlântico*, 1 (1942), 163-6.
A general survey of Gil Vicente's theater, with emphasis on the *Visitação*, and a mention of recent stagings of Vicentine works by several companies.

Gil Vicente and Other Figures

556   Campos, Agostinho de. 'Gil Vicente e Camões.' *RFLUL*, VII (1941), 346-63.

557   Castelo-Branco, Fernando. 'Gil Vicente e Sá de Miranda.' *Boletim Cultural da Câmara Municipal do Porto*, XXIX (1966), 447-67.

558   Cidade, Hernâni. 'No centenário de Gil Vicente: homenagem de Camões a Mestre Gil.' *Colóquio*, 36 (December 1965), 45-8.

559 Cortez Pinto, Américo. 'Gil Vicente, Camões e os janotas.' *Colóquio*, 18 (May 1962), 61-4.

560 Crespo, Firmino. 'Gil Vicente e Amato Lusitano em Santarém.' *Colóquio*, 47 (February 1968), 55-6.

561 Gomes, Alberto F. 'Gil Vicente, D. Diogo Pinheiro e os judeus.' *Ocidente*, LXX (1966), 18-24.
Maintains that Gil Vicente was notably tolerant toward the Jews.

562 ——. 'Gil Vicente na obra de Frédéric Ozanam.' *Mensário de Casas do Povo*, 235 (1966), 12-13.

563 M[achado], J[osé] P[edro]. 'Gil Vicente e o Infante D. Pedro.' *RdP*, XXVIII (1963), 400-4.

564 Oliveira, Joaquim de. 'Dona Leonor e Gil Vicente.' *Autores*, 2 (1958), 13-14.

565 Ramalho, Américo da Costa. 'Cataldo Sículo e Gil Vicente.' *Colóquio*, 49 (June 1968), 62-3.

566 Stinson, Robert R. 'Gil Vicente, Erasmus, and a Legend.' *RomN*, XIII (1971-2), 535-40.
Disproves the myth that Erasmus had learned Portuguese in order to read Gil Vicente.

Gil Vicente, Middle Ages and Renaissance

567 Ferrario de Orduna, Lilia. 'La adoración de los pastores. II: el paso al Renacimiento en Gil Vicente y en las artes visuales.' *Filología*, XI (1965), 41-64.

568 Houwens Post, Hendrik. 'As obras de Gil Vicente como elo de transição entre o drama medieval e o teatro do Renascimento.' Trans. Luís-Crespo Fabião. *Arquivos do Centro Cultural Português*, IX (1975), 101-21.

569 Silva, Rui Rosas da & J.B. Mota Amaral. 'Gil Vicente, poeta medieval voltado para o futuro. Entrevista com o Prof. Enzio di Poppa.' *Rumo*, 107 (January 1966), 61-4.

570* Sletsjøe, Leif. 'Gil Vicente (1465-1965): Dramatiker på grensen mellom Middelalder og Renessance' [Gil Vicente (1465-1965): Dramatist on the Border between the Middle Ages and the Renaissance]. *Minerva's Kvartalsskrift* (1966), 1-15.
See also above, no. 192.

Gil Vicente's Modernity and Universality

571 'Actualidade de Gil Vicente. Debate gravado.' *TeM*, 33 (December 1965), 1147-81.

572 Alge, Carlos d'. 'Universalidade do teatro vicentino.' *Clã*, XVII (1965), 115-31.

573* Brasil, Reis [José Gomes Bras]. 'Actualidade e perenidade do teatro de Gil Vicente.' *PRJ* (17 July 1963).

574 Brito Chaves, Irma de. 'A atualidade no teatro de Gil Vicente.' *Alfa*, 15 (1969), 241-51.

575 Chaves, Flávio Loureiro. 'Actualidade de Gil Vicente.' *BGPL*, 4 (January 1966), 6-9.

576 Gonçalves, Ana Maria. 'A modernidade do teatro de Gil Vicente.' *Estudos de Castelo Branco*, 15 (1965), 120-9.

577 Jesus, Eduíno de. 'Actualidade de Gil Vicente.' *Autores*, 14 (1961), 25-6.

578 Rebello, Luiz Francisco. 'Actualidade de Gil Vicente.' *Seara Nova*, XLIV (1965), 208.
See above, no. 356.

579 Saraiva, António José & Maria Teresa Rita. 'Diálogo sobre a actualidade crítica de Gil Vicente entre um historiador e uma jovem autora teatral.' *Vértice*, XXV (1965), 715-24.

Textual and Linguistic Aspects

580 Capela e Silva, J.A. 'A linguagem rústica: a propósito das interjeições *uxtix*, de Gil Vicente, e *oxte*, de Cervantes.' *Ocidente*, XXXIV (1948), 115-19.

581* Castro, Aníbal de. 'As edições e os textos de Gil Vicente.' *ComP* (8 June 1965).

582 Fernandes, A. Ferrand de Almeida. 'Notícia sobre o exemplar da *Copilaçam de todalas obras de Gil Vicente*, da impressão de 1562, existente na Biblioteca do Palácio Nacional de Mafra.' *Arquivo de Bibliografia Portuguesa*, III (1957), 10-15.

583 Maler, Bertil. 'Duas nótulas vicentinas.' *Ibero-Romanskt*, I (1966), 50-6.
1: "Por vida de Semaforá" (*Barca do Inferno*). 2: "Não ha hi favo de mel / tão doce como a preguiça" (*Juiz da Beira*).
Reviews:
.1. Iacob M. Hassán, *Sefarad*, XXVII (1967), 228.
.2. Manuel Augusto Rodrigues, *RPF*, XV (1969), 301-6.

584 Monteverdi, Angelo. 'Bilinguismo letterario.' *BdF*, XIX (1960), 87-93.

584A Pestana, Sebastião. 'Apontamentos gilvicentinos.' *BMSLP*, IX (1958), 40-1, 226-7.
Philological notes on several plays.

585 ——. 'Pequena amostra do *Dicionário de Gil Vicente*.' *Ocidente*, LXXXI (1971), 370-87.

585A Piel, José M. 'Sobre alguns termos rústicos da linguagem de Gil Vicente.'
Aufsätze zur Portugiesischen Kulturgeschichte, XIII (1974-5), 150-6.
(1. *samica-samicas*. 2. *pardicas*. 3. *nega-nego*. 4. *sonca-soncas*. 5. *abém*.
6. *módão, crédão, saibão, bérbão*)

586 Révah, I.S. 'Quelques mots du lexique de Gil Vicente.' *Revista Brasileira
de Filologia*, II (1956), 143-54.
(*burrela, deteira, dix, zote*).

587 Rossi, Giuseppe Carlo. 'Il problema dei testi di Gil Vicente.' *Filologia
Romanza*, II (1956), 314-23.

588 —. 'Text- und Sprach-probleme Gil Vicentes im Lichte der neuesten
Forschung.' *Neuphilologische Mitteilungen*,LVIII (1957), 196-206.

589 Sletsjфe, Leif. 'Dos fenómenos lingüísticos en la obra dramática de Gil
Vicente: diptongo *oi* por *ou*; desinencia verbal *-ade*.' *RJ*, XVII (1966),
301-22.

590 —. 'Los posesivos *nuesso* y *vuesso* en el español de Gil Vicente.' *RJ*,
XVI (1965), 274-89.

591 Vieira, Manuel Higino. 'Ementas gilvicentinas.' *RdP*, XXXIV (1969),
262-7.
On the etymology of *sobejo, tomar, afogar, heréu, há já dius*, all of which
occur in the *Auto da Alma*.

Classification

592* Rebello, Luiz Francisco. 'Esboço de classificação do teatro de Gil Vicente.'
ComP (8 June 1965).

593 Tomlins, Jack E. 'Una nota sobre la clasificación de los dramas de Gil
Vicente.' *Duquesne Hispanic Review*, III (1964), 115-31; IV (1965), 1-16.

Characters

593A Barata, José Oliveira. 'O vilão às avessas do seu mundo. Para um estudo
do vilão vicentino.' *Biblos*, LI (1975), 93-123.

594 Coelho, Nelly Novaes. 'As alcoviteiras vicentinas.' *Alfa*, 4 (1963), 83-105.

594A —. 'As "mediadoras" vicentinas.' *ESPSL*, 457 (4 December 1965), 4.

595* Delgado, Rafael. 'El poeta Gil Vicente y la nana.' *El Universal* (18
September 1954).

596 Moser, Gerald M. 'An Index to the Characters in the Dramatic Works of Gil
Vicente.' *Theatre Documentation*, II, 1-2 (Fall 1969-Spring 1970), 19-47.

Comedy

597 Leonardos, Stella. 'Das comédias de Gil Vicente.' *Comentário*, VI (1965),
231-5.

598   Ramalho, Américo da Costa. 'Alguns aspectos do cómico vicentino.' *Biblos*, XLI (1965), 5-33.

599   Révah, I.S. 'La *comédia* dans l'oeuvre de Gil Vicente.' *BHTP*, II (1951), 1-39.
Reprinted as no. 358A.

600   Saviotti, Gino. 'Gil Vicente poeta cómico.' *BHTP*, II (1951), 181-211.

The Lyrical Element

600A   Cidade, Hernâni. 'O poeta Gil Vicente.' *ESPSL*, 457 (4 December 1965), 6.

601   Di Poppa, Enzio. 'Gil Vicente, compiuto poeta.' *Convivium*, XX (1952), 216-32.

602   Lemos, Ester de. 'A propósito de Gil Vicente poeta lírico.' *Panorama*, 13 (1965), 9-14.

603   Reckert, Stephen. 'La lírica de Gil Vicente: estructura y estilo.' *CH*, 280-2 (October-November 1973), 463-83. With an Appendix of the texts of the poems cited, pp. 483-86.
Revised version included in no. 285A, above.

604   Sánchez, Alberto. 'Os poemas castelhanos de Gil Vicente.' *Vértice*, XXV (1965), 727-32.

Music

605   Bonito, Porfírio Augusto Rebelo. 'Aspectos musicais dos autos de Gil Vicente.' *Gazeta Musical*, VIII (1958), 84-5.

606   —. 'Nótulas de etnografia musical. XVIII: um texto musical de Gil Vicente.' *Gazeta Musical*, IV (1954), 317-20.
Aires Rosado's serenade ("Si dormís, doncella") in *Quem tem farelos?*.

606A   —. 'Novos aspectos musicais dos autos de Gil Vicente.' *Gazeta Musical*, VIII (1958), 100-1.

607   Kiefer, Bruno. 'A música portuguêsa na época de Gil Vicente.' *BGPL*, 4 (January 1966), 39-44.

608   Oliveira, Flávio. 'Música espanhola e Gil Vicente.' *BGPL*, 4 (January 1966), 45-53.

Ethnography and Folklore

609   Chaves, Luís. 'Gil Vicente. Aspectos etnográficos na sua obra poética e dramática.' *Ethnos*, V (1966), 169-87.

610   —. 'Nos domínios da etnografia portuguesa.' *Ocidente*, LXIV (1963), 275-83.
Bagpipes and timbrels in Gil Vicente and in folklore.

611   Dias, Jaime Lopes. 'Etnografia da Beira. Festas populares, ciclo do Natal:

a Adoração dos pastores.' *Ocidente*, XI (1940), 395-407.
Traces parallels between the Adoration of the shepherds, as practised in Beira, and Gil Vicente's *Auto pastoril castelhano*.

612 Joiner, Virginia & Eunice Joiner Gates. 'Proverbs in the Works of Gil Vicente.' *PMLA*, LVII (1942), 57-73.

612A* Melo, Maria da Graça Rios de. 'Literatura oral e teatro popular.' *Minas Gerais. Suplemento Literário* (29 November 1975), pp. 4-5.

613 Ramos, Maria Micaela. 'Gil Vicente e o folclore.' *Boletim Cultural da Junta Distrital de Lisboa*, 57-8 (1962), 191-200; 59-60 (1963), 249-66; 61-2 (1964), 337-52; 63-4 (1965), 353-60; 65-6 (1966), 305-14; 67-8 (1967), 329-34; 69-70 (1968), 271-86; 71-2 (1969), 249-77; 73-4 (1970), 253-8; 75-8 (1971-2), 211-21.

614 Santos, Júlio Eduardo dos. 'Nota gil-vicentina de interesse olisiponense.' *Olisipo*, XXXIX (1966), 38-42.

615 Soromenho, Paulo Caratão. 'Caminhadas lisboetas de Gil Vicente.' *Olisipo*, XXXIX (1966), 11-37.

Religious and Related Matters

616 Barbosa, Jorge de Morais. 'Gil Vicente e os seus diabos.' *BMSLP*, VI, 1 (January 1955), 1-9; 2 (February 1955), 53-67.

617* Carvalho, Joaquim de. 'Os sermões de Gil Vicente e a arte de pregar.' *PRJ* (1 June 1949).
See also above, nos 242, 287.

618 Cury, Jorge. 'Gil Vicente e a teoria do livre arbítrio.' *Ocidente*, LXIX (1965), 158-63.

619* Deniz-Jacinto. 'Na esteira dos diabos de Gil Vicente.' *ComP* (8 June 1965).

620 Gil Álvarez, Felipe. 'Navidad en el teatro de Castilla.' *Haz*, 9 (December 1943), 24-5.
Includes Gil Vicente.

621 Houwens Post, Hendrik. 'Gil Vicente proto-érasmien.' *Caravelle*, 9 (1967), 97-108.
Ideological parallels between Erasmus and Gil Vicente.
Review:
.1. E.P., *RdP*, XXXIII (1968), 399-400.

622 Lopes, A. da Costa. 'Gil Vicente e o Papa.' *Cenáculo*, V (1965-6), 3-20.

623 Martins, Mário. 'Gil Vicente e o texto dos Livros de Horas.' *CoL*, 3 (September 1971), 29-36.

624 ——. 'S. Pero Gonçalvez, O.P., o "Corpo Santo" e Gil Vicente.' *Lusitania Sacra*, VIII (1970), 39-55.

Gil Vicente refers to S. Pero Gonçalvez in the storm scene of the *Triunfo do Inverno.*

625* Montalegre, Duarte de. 'Gil Vicente e a liberdade espiritual no seu tempo.' *PRJ* (18 May 1960).

626 Oliveira, Zacarias de. 'Deus e o homem em Gil Vicente.' *Lumen*, XXIX (1965), 441-6, 522-9.

627* P., P. e S. 'Gil Vicente e o erasmismo.' *O Concelho da Murtosa* (30 November 1940).

628 Pimenta, Alberto. 'O conceito do diabo na Bíblia e em Gil Vicente.' *Ocidente*, LXIX (1965), 231-47.

629 Révah, I.S. 'La Censure inquisitoriale et les oeuvres de Gil Vicente.' *BHTP*, I (1950), 117-19.

629A* ——. 'Le Théâtre religieux de Gil Vicente.' *Annuaire de l'École Pratique des Hautes Études. IVᵉ Section (Paris), 1960-1961* (1961), 73-4; *1961-1962* (1962), 86-7; *1962-1963* (1963), 143-4; *1963-1964* (1964), 191-3.

630 Sampaio, Jorge de. 'Dramaturgia mariana em Gil Vicente.' *Panorama*, 12 (1964), 28-32.

631 Sano, Yasuhiko. 'Gil Vicente no Gikyoku ni okeru Akukozo' [Images of Evil in Gil Vicente's Drama] . *Sophia*, XXI (1972), 46-58.

632 Vasconcelos, Reinaldo de. 'Gil Vicente e a sociedade eclesiástica de mil e quinhentos.' *Brotéria*, LXXIII (1961), 506-33.

Interpretation

633 Andrews, J. Richard. 'The Harmonizing Perspective of Gil Vicente.' *BCom*, XI, 2 (Fall 1959), 1-5.

634 Atkinson, William C. '*Comedias, tragicomedias* and *farças* in Gil Vicente.' *BdF*, XI (1950), 268-80.

635 Tomlins, Jack E. 'Toward an Aesthetic of Gil Vicente's Drama.' *Journal of the American Portuguese Cultural Society*, II (1968), 42-64.

636 Wardropper, Bruce W. 'Approaching the Metaphysical Sense of Gil Vicente's Chivalric Tragicomedies.' *BCom*, XVI, 1 (Spring 1964), 1-9.

Miscellaneous

637 Abreu, José de. 'Camilo Castelo Branco: notas em livros.' *RdP*, XXX (1965), 418-27.
Castelo Branco's handwritten notes in his copy of Gil Vicente's *Obras.*

638* Aguiar e Silva, Vitor Manuel de. 'Aspectos de imagem em Gil Vicente.' *Diário de Notícias* (20 August 1965).
Also published in *ESPSL*, 457 (4 December 1965), 3.

639 Albuquerque, Luís de. 'A astrologia e Gil Vicente.' *Arquivos do Centro Cultural Português*, III (1971), 54-75.
A more elaborate version of his 'Gil Vicente e a astrologia'. *Vértice*, XXV (1965), 817-23.

640* Alegria, José Augusto. 'Missão de Gil Vicente.' *Suplemento de "Novidades"*, 75 (9 August 1965).

641 Anon. 'Cronologia de Gil Vicente.' *Dionysos*, X, 12 (September 1965), 51-8.

642* Arruda, Virgílio. 'Gil Vicente em Santarém.' *Correio do Ribatejo* (7 & 14 August 1965).

643 Berardinelli, Cleonice. 'Linhas mestras da literatura portuguesa.' *Ocidente*, LXXXI (1971), 33-9.
Affinities between Fernão Lopes, Gil Vicente, Luís de Camões and three modern writers.

644* Cidade, Hernâni. 'Gil Vicente e *A diferença entre os nascidos.' PRJ* (24 March 1965).

644A Costa, Aida. 'Gil Vicente e o mundo clássico.' *ESPSL*, 457 (4 December 1965), 2.

645* Di Poppa, Enzio. 'Gil Vicente, poeta social. Um trecho da introdução da versão italiana das suas obras.' *PRJ* (25 November 1953).
See above, no. 189.

646 Dória, António Álvaro. 'Um gilvicentista devotado e esquecido.' *GilV*, XVII (1966), 69-85.   On Aubrey F. G. Bell.

646A* Gomes, A. Figueira. 'O culto de Gil Vicente em Espanha.' *Jornal de Letras e Artes* (24 July 1963).

647 Gonçalves, Joaquim Cerqueira. 'A dialéctica do optimismo e do pessimismo na obra de Gil Vicente.' *Itinerarium*, XII (1966), 68-78.

648 Hess, Rainer. 'Die Naturauffassung Gil Vicentes.' *Aufsätze zur Portugiesischen Kulturgeschichte*, V (1965), 1-64.
Review:
.1. H. Kröll, *RJ*, XIX (1968), 377.

649 Mendes, João. 'Gil Vicente sobre-realista.' *Brotéria*, LXXXVI (1968), 329-50, 456-75.

650 Pestana, Sebastião. 'Estudos gilvicentinos.' *RdP*, VIII (1945), 49-60; IX (1946), 32-5; XII (1947), 34-8, 75-8; XIII (1948), 159-63; XIV (1949), 250-3; XV (1950), 48-54, 137-41; XVI (1951), 327-8; XIX (1954), 221-4, 241-5; XX (1955), 13-16; XXI (1956), 121-6, 175-6, 193-6, 222-4, 254-5, 302-12; XXII (1957), 289-94; XXIII (1958), 501-6; XXIV (1959), 183-6, 410-14; XXV (1960), 362-71; XXVI (1961), 363-7; XXVIII (1963), 445-54; XXIX (1964), 101-3, 469-73; XXX (1965), 14-18.

651   —. 'Silva gilvicentina.' *Ocidente*, LXXX (1971), 425-34.

652   Rebello, Luiz Francisco. 'As duas faces do teatro vicentino.' *Espiral*, II (1965), 79-81.
Gil Vicente's theater is characterized by dualism on many planes (themes, structure, diction, etc.). See above, no. 356.

653   —. 'Introdução à dramaturgia vicentina.' *Dionysos*, X, 12 (September 1965), 5-15.

654   Reckert, Stephen. 'Marginália vicentina: três apostilas.' *RFLUL*, VIII (1964), 274-80.
I: "hûa visitaçam que o autor fez" (questions the belief that the dramatist himself acted in the *Auto da visitação*). II: "A obra de devaçam seguinte" (refers to the *Auto pastoril castelhano* rather than the *Visitação*). III: "Que me hizo ñifrerias" (*Comédia do viúvo*: "ñifrerias" is the compositor's error for "niñerías"). Revised version included in no. 285A, above.

654A   Rossi, Giuseppe Carlo. 'Relendo Gil Vicente.' *ESPSL*, 457 (4 December 1965), 6.

655   Rougle, William. 'A importância do ouro e das pedras preciosas na obra de Gil Vicente.' Trans. Ricardo Paiva. *Ocidente*, Número especial (1974), 7-17.

656*   Sampaio, Nuno de. 'Gil Vicente e os seus leitores.' *PRJ* (18 November 1964).

657*   Soares, A.J. 'Coimbra e Gil Vicente.' *PRJ* (27 June 1965).

658   Sten, Holger. 'Uma opinião dinamarquesa sobre Gil Vicente.' *Ocidente*, LXIX (1965), 15-16.
Suggests that if Gil Vicente's poetry is to be fully appreciated, it has to be read in the original.

658A   Torres, Alberto Pinheiro. 'Duas glórias da ourivesaria: Santo Elói e Gil Vicente.' *Ourivesaria Portuguesa*, 1 & 2 (1948), 15-19, 63-5.
Supports the identification of Gil Vicente, the dramatist, with Gil Vicente, the goldsmith. Quotes relevant passages from the *Farsa dos almocreves* and describes the Custódia de Belém.

659*   Ventura, Augusta Faria Gersão. 'Gil Vicente e a nossa epopéia marítima.' *Gazeta de Coimbra* (15 May 1941).

660   —. 'Referências de Gil Vicente ao Brasil.' *Brasília*, I (1942), 123-32.

661   Ventura, Francisco. 'Gil Vicente poeta de Portugal.' *Sulco*, I (1965), 530-66.

662*   Vieira, Manuel Higino. 'Dificuldade na cronologia das obras de Gil Vicente.' *A Huíla* (12 February 1969).

Critical Studies

Briefer Mentions

663   Altman, Leonard. 'Music in the Early Spanish Theatre.' *American Record Guide*, XXVII (1961), 542-5, 591-2.

664   De Chasca, Edmund V. 'The Phonology of the Speech of the Negroes in Early Spanish Drama.' *HR*, XIV (1946), 322-39.

665   Deyermond, Alan D. 'El hombre salvaje en la novela sentimental.' *Filología*, X (1964), 97-111.
       Reprinted in shorter and somewhat modified form in *Actas del Segundo Congreso internacional de hispanistas celebrado en Nijmegen del 20 al 25 de agosto de 1965*, ed. Jaime Sánchez-Romeralo& Norbert Poulussen (Nijmegen: Instituto Español de la Universidad de Nimega, 1967), pp. 265-72.

666   Frenk Alatorre, Margit. 'Dignificación de la lírica popular en el Siglo de Oro.' *Anuario de Letras*, II (1962), 27-54.

667   —. 'Glosas de tipo popular en la antigua lírica.' *NRFH*, XII (1958), 301-34.

668   García Gómez, Emilio. 'La canción famosa *Calvi vi calvi / Calvi aravi.*' *Al-Andalus*, XXI (1956), 1-18, 215-16.
       To be found in *Dom Duardos*, too.

669   Gillet, Joseph E. '*Apiahá.*' *RPhi*, V (1951-2), 316-18.
       Defines the word and traces its history. *Apiahá* is also found in the *Floresta de enganos*.

670   —. '*Las ochavas en cadena*: A Proverb in Rodrigo de Cota and Diego Sánchez de Badajoz.' *RPhi*, VI (1952-3) 264-7.
       Discusses also the expression "tener ochavas la fiesta" to be found in *Dom Duardos*.

671   Jason, Howard M. 'The Language of the Negro in the Early Spanish Drama.' *College Language Association Journal*, X (1967), 333-40.

672   Lihani, John. 'Lucas Fernández and the Evolution of the Shepherd's Family Pride in Early Spanish Drama.' *HR*, XXV (1957), 252-63.

673   —. 'Some Notes on *sayagués.*' *Hispania*, XLI (1958), 165-9.

674   Lovett, Gabriel H. 'The Churchman in the Spanish Drama before Lope de Vega.' *BCom*, IV, 2 (Fall 1952), 10-13.

675   —. 'The Hermit in the Spanish Drama before Lope de Vega.' *MLJ*, XXXV (1951), 340-55.
       Includes a discussion of the hermit, as character, in the *Auto dos Reis Magos, Comédia sobre a divisa da cidade de Coimbra, Amadis de Gaula, Tragicomédia pastoril da Serra da Estrêla, Inês Pereira*.

676 Luz, Marilina dos Santos. 'Fórmulas de tratamento no português arcaico. Subsídios para o seu estudo.' *RPF*, VII (1956), 251-363; VIII (1957), 187-252; IX (1958-9), 55-157.

676A Martins, José V. de Pina. 'Sobre o conceito do humanismo e alguns aspectos histórico-doutrinários da cultura renascentista.' *Arquivos do Centro Cultural Português*, II (1970), 192-281.
On Gil Vicente, pp. 264-71 *et passim*.

677 Martins, Mário. 'A rainha Dona Leonor e os livros.' *Brotéria*, LXVII (1958), 249-57.

678 Myers, Oliver T. 'Church Latin Elements in *Sayagués*.' *RomN*, IV (1962-3), 166-8.

679 Quadros, António. 'Teatro português, teatro universal.' *Espiral*, II (1965), 3-16.
The first Christian dramatist is Gil Vicente, who deserves to be considered the Aeschylus of the new cycle of civilization.

680 Ribeiro, António Lopes. 'O preconceito "intelectual" contra o teatro português.' *Atlântico*, 3 (1943), 192-4.

681 Rocha, Andrée Crabbé. 'Ébauches dramatiques dans le *Cancioneiro geral*.' *BHTP*, II (1951), 113-50.

682 Ruggerio, Michael J. 'Dramatic Conventions in the Sixteenth Century Spanish Theatre.' *BCom*, XXIII (1971), 36-9.
Touches upon the use of monologue in *Dom Duardos* and *Cassandra*.

683 Salazar, Adolfo. 'Music in the Primitive Spanish Theatre before Lope de Vega.' *Papers of the American Musicological Society* (1940), 94-108.

684 Sloman, Albert E. 'The Phonology of Moorish Jargon in the Works of Early Spanish Dramatists and Lope de Vega.' *MLR*, XLIV (1949), 207-17.

685 Stegagno Picchio, Luciana. '*Arremedilho*. Di un presunto componimento drammatico giullaresco alle origini del teatro portoghese.' *AION-SR*, II (1960), 31-45.
Reappeared, in revised form, as 'O filão joglaresco no teatro medieval português: o problema do *arremedilho*' in her 'Quatro lições sobre o teatro português.' *EIP*, XXVIII (1967), 69-85. Was later reprinted, in Italian version, in her *Ricerche sul teatro portoghese* (see above, no. 369), pp. 39-62.

686 Stern, Charlotte. '*Sayago* and *sayagués* in Spanish History and Literature.' *HR*, XXIX (1961), 217-37.

687 —. 'Some New Thoughts on the Early Spanish Drama.' *BCom*, XVIII, 1 (Spring 1966), 14-19.

688 ——. 'The Early Spanish Drama: From Medieval Ritual to Renaissance Art.' *Renaissance Drama*, VI (1973), 177-201.

689 Vieira, Primo. 'Sobre os autos de Anchieta.' *CoL*, 16 (November 1973), 66-8.
Some comparative references to Gil Vicente.

690 Webber, Edwin J. '*Arte mayor* in the Early Spanish Drama.' *RPhi*, V (1951-2), 49-60.

691 Weber de Kurlat, Frida. 'El dialecto sayagués y los críticos.' *Filología*, I (1949), 43-50.

692 ——. 'El tipo cómico del negro en el teatro prelopesco: fonética.' *Filología*, VIII (1962), 139-68.

693 ——. 'Latinismos arrusticados en el sayagués.' *NRFH*, I (1947), 166-70.

694 ——. 'Sobre el negro como tipo cómico en el teatro español del siglo XVI.' *RPhi*, XVII (1963-4), 380-91.

ii. Individual Works

O monólogo do vaqueiro (1502)

695* Lopes, Francisco Fernandes. '*O monólogo do vaqueiro* de Gil Vicente.' *PRJ* (14 May 1952).

696 See also above, nos 267, 555, 654.

Auto da Índia (1509)

696A Busnardo, Maria Salete. 'Notas para montagem da farsa chamada *Auto da Índia*.' *Arquivos*, II (1973), 23-56.

697 Castelo-Branco, Maria dos Remédios. 'Significado do cómico do *Auto da Índia*.' *Ocidente*, LXX (1966), 129-36.

698* Chaves, Luís. 'O *Auto da Índia* e a sugestão poética de uma casa quinhentista da cidade.' *Suplemento de "Novidades"*, no. 66 (7 June 1965).

699 McGrady, Donald. 'The Italian Sources of Gil Vicente's *Auto da Índia*.' *RPhi*, XXX (1976-7), 321-30.
Boccaccio's *Decamerone* (VIII, 7) and Masuccio Salernitano's *Il novellino* (*novella* 29).

700 Moser, Gerald M. 'A volta do marido.' *Vértice*, XXV (1965), 795-8.

700A* Teles, Jorge de Sousa. 'Uma farsa chamada *Auto da Índia*.' *Arquivos*, I (1971), 18-27.

Auto pastoril castelhano (1509)

701 Lihani, John. 'Personal Elements in Gil Vicente's *Auto pastoril castellano*.' *HR*, XXXVII (1969), 297-303.
Internal evidence leads the author to believe that both Gil Vicente and

Lucas Fernández acted in the play's first performance.

702   See also above, nos 547, 567, 611, 654.

Auto dos Reis Magos (1510)

703   See above, nos 547, 675.

O velho da horta (1512)

704   Lucas, João de Almeida. 'Notas para uma edição de Gil Vicente. *O velho da horta.' Ocidente*, XVII (1942), 325-34.

705   Nogueira-Martins, Carlos. 'A propósito de la *Humanidade e grandeza do "Velho da horta".' RomN*, VIII (1966-7), 96-7.
       See above, no. 273.

706   Oliveira, Joaquim de. '*O velho da horta* de Gil Vicente.' *Autores*, VII (1964), 27-8.

707   Santilli, Maria Aparecida. 'Reflexões sôbre *O velho da horta.' ESPSL*, 457 (4 December 1965), 5.

708   See also above, nos 273, 369.

Auto dos Quatro Tempos (1513)

709   See above, no. 303.

Auto da sibila Cassandra (1513)

710   Hart, Thomas R. 'Gil Vicente's *Auto de la Sibila Casandra.' HR*, XXVI (1958), 35-51.

711   Révah, I.S. 'L'*Auto de la Sibylle Cassandre* de Gil Vicente.' *HR*, XXVII (1959), 167-93.

712   Sieber, Harry. '*Ordo Profetarum* and Comedy in the *Auto de la Sibila Casandra.' BCom*, XXVII (1975), 1-5.

713   Weber de Kurlat, Frida. 'Gil Vicente y Diego Sánchez de Badajoz. A propósito del *Auto da sebila Casandra* y de la *Farsa del juego de cañas.' Filología*, IX (1963), 119-62.

714   See also above, nos 329, 336, 368, 414, 547, 682.

Exortação da guerra (1514)

715   Lucas, João de Almeida. 'Notas para uma edição crítica de Gil Vicente. *Tragicomédia da exortação da guerra.' Ocidente*, XX (1943), 49-60.

Quem tem farelos? (1515)

716   See above, nos 256, 297, 606.

Auto de Mofina Mendes (1515)

717   Cascudo, Luís da Câmara. 'Viagem com Mofina Mendes, ou da imaginação determinante.' *Memórias da Academia das Ciências de Lisboa*,

IX (1966), 45-62.

718   Magalhães, António Dias de. 'O significado do auto vicentino da *Mofina Mendes.' Brotéria*, XXXIX (1944), 173-95, 303-24.

719   Révah, I.S. 'Un tema de Torres Naharro y de Gil Vicente.' *NRFH*, VII (1953), 417-25.
       Annunciation in the *Diálogo de Nascimiento* and the *Auto de Mofina Mendes*.

720   See also above, nos 242, 262.

Autos das Barcas (1517, 1518, 1519)

721   Conde Júnior, B.Guerra.'Gil Vicente y *La Celestina.' ELit*, 343 (7 May 1966), 8-9.
       The *Barca do Inferno* is like a version of *Celestina.*

722   David, Pierre. 'Notes sur deux motifs introduits par Gil Vicente dans l'*Auto da embarcação da Glória.' BEP*, X (1945), 189-203.
       The motifs of the two ships and the saving of the souls after death through Divine Mercy, and their antecedents.

723   Lyday, Leon F. 'The *Barcas* and the *Compadecida*: *Autos* Past and Present.' *L-BR*, XI (1974), 84-8.
       Structural parallels between the *Burcas* and Ariano Suassuna's play.

724   Mulertt, Werner. 'Volkstümlich-Katholisches bei Gil Vicente. Die St. Gregorsmesse in der Barken-Trilogie.' *VKR*, XIV (1941), 149-68.
       Review:
       .1. W. Hering, *ZRP*, LXIII (1943), 474-5.

725   Pestana, Sebastião. 'Apontamentos gilvicentinos.' *BMSLP*, IX (1958), 3-7.
       Commentary on the Bishop scene of the *Barca da Glória.*

726   Pinto, Milton José. '*Barcas* vicentinas: ideologia de uma época.' *Vozes*, LXIII (1969), 245-52.

727   Quintela, Paulo. 'Motivgeschichtliche Betrachtungen zu den *Barcas* des Gil Vicente.' *RF*, LVI (1942), 359-63.

728   Ventura, Augusta Faria Gersão. 'O "côco" da *Barca do Purgatório* de Gil Vicente e o "jasmim" dos *Lusíadas* e da lírica de Camões.' *Liceus de Portugal*, 29 (1943), 2329-34.
       On the etymology of *côco*.

729   See also above, nos 303, 306, 308, 319, 352-3, 371, 421, 543, 583.

Auto da Alma (1518)

730   Ayala, Walmir. 'Uma adaptação de Gil Vicente.' *Dionysos*, X, 12 (September 1965), 62-8.

Introduces his "free adaptation" of the *Auto da Alma* (see no. 107, above) and explains the procedure he has followed.

731 Carvalho, António Pinto de. 'Um equívoco de Gil Vicente. Análise de um passo do *Auto da Alma*.' *BHS*, XXVII (1950), 33-6.
St Augustine's prayer, toward the end of the play.

732 Gomes, Alberto F. 'Características do *Auto da Alma* e fé de Gil Vicente.' *Ocidente*, LXIX (1965), 17-21.

732A Lourenço, M.S. 'O homem como planta no *Auto da Alma* de Gil Vicente.' *Boletim Cultural da Junta Distrital de Lisboa*, Série III, 81 (1975), 99-117.

733 Moser, Fernando de Mello. 'Liturgia e iconografia na interpretação do *Auto da Alma*.' *RFLUL*, VI (1962), 86-112.
Also reissued independently (Lisboa: Faculdade de Letras, 1966), 30 pp.
Review:
.1. A.R., *Brotéria*, LXXXVI (1968), 280.

734 See also above, nos 231, 255, 316, 350, 591, and below, no. 785.

Auto da Fama (1520)

735 See above, no. 323.

Côrtes de Júpiter (1521)

736 Machado, José Pedro. 'A fala da moura das *Cortes de Júpiter* de Gil Vicente.' *RdP*, XXX (1965), 402-16.
Reprinted, in revised form, from the *RFLUL*, V (1938), 221-50.

737 Pestana, Sebastião. 'Estudos gilvicentinos. XXXVI. Contribuição para o estudo das *Côrtes de Júpiter* de Gil Vicente.' *Ocidente*, LXIX (1965), 205-18.

Comédia de Rubena (1521)

738 David-Peyre, Yvonne. 'La *Comédia de Rubena*. Une pièce insolite de Gil Vicente.' *BEP*, XXXII (1971), 11-27.

739 Hart, Thomas R. 'The Dramatic Unity of Gil Vicente's *Comédia de Rubena*.' *BHS*, XLVI (1969), 97-108.

Tragicomédia de Dom Duardos (1522)

739A Fontes, Manuel da Costa. 'D. Duardos in the Portuguese Oral Tradition.' *RPhi*, XXX (1976-7), 589-608.

740 Hart, Thomas R. 'Courtly Love in Gil Vicente's *Don Duardos*.' *RomN*, II (1960-1), 103-6.

741 Orduna, Germán. 'Observaciones al texto de la *Tragicomedia de Don Duardos* (a propósito de una representación reciente).' *Filología*, XIII (1968-9), 289-94.

742   Rivers, Elias L. 'The Unity of *Don Duardos*.' *MLN*, LXXVI (1961), 759-66.

743   See also above, nos 300-1, 324, 348, 374, 447, 530, 636, 668, 670, 682.

Auto de Inês Pereira (1523)

744   Álvarez Blázquez, Xosé María. 'Gil Vicente e Galicia. I: O conto das dúas lousas.' *Grial*, II (1964), 235-9.
On a passage in *Inês Pereira.*

745   Artola, G.T. & W.A. Eichengreen. 'A Judeo-Portuguese Passage in the *Farça de Inês Pereira* of Gil Vicente.' *MLN*, LXIII (1948), 342-6.

746   Hart, Thomas R. 'La estructura dramática del *Auto de Inês Pereira*.' *NRFH*, XVIII (1965-6), 160-5.

747   See also above, nos 256, 349, 675.

Auto pastoril português (1523)

748   Lucas, João de Almeida. 'Notas para uma edição de Gil Vicente. *Auto em pastoril português*.' *Ocidente*, XVI (1942), 455-64.

Tragicomédia de Amadis de Gaula (1523)

749   See above, nos 324, 470, 636, 675.

Comédia do viúvo (1524)

750   See above, nos 324, 337, 375, 654.

Frágua de Amor (1524)

751   See above, no. 353.

Farsa dos físicos (1524)

752*   Brasil, Reis [José Gomes Bras] . 'A *Farsa dos físicos* e a crítica ao clero.' *PRJ* (18 January 1961).

753*   —. 'A *Farsa dos físicos* e a crítica vicentina.' *PRJ* (30 November 1960).

754*   —. 'A *Farsa dos físicos*: obra-prima de crítica social.' *PRJ* (16 November 1960).

755*   Granada, Novais. 'Mestre Gil, físico.' *Suplemento Semanal do "Diário de Lisboa"* (26 August 1965).

756   Pedro, António. 'Acerca do que ninguém leu, ou não quis ler, na *Farça dos físicos* de Gil Vicente.' *TeM*, 33 (December 1965), 1141-6.

757   Ventura, Augusta Faria Gersão. 'A "Arte de Leste a Oeste" nas obras de Gil Vicente: data do *Auto dos físicos*.' *Liceus de Portugal*, 5 (1941), 358-70.
On the basis of internal astrological evidence, she concludes that the play belongs to 1524.

758   See also above, nos 256, 299.

O Juiz da Beira (1525 or 1526)

759   Jesus, Eduíno de. '*O Juiz da Beira* de Gil Vicente e o direito do seu tempo.' *Autores*, 13 (1961), 19-21.

760   See also above, nos 256, 583.

Auto da feira (1526)

761   Lucas, João de Almeida. 'Notas para uma edição de Gil Vicente. *Auto da feira*.' *Portucale*, XV (1942), 83-100.

762   Ribeiro, Mário de Sampayo. 'A missa da meia-noite do ano 1527 no Paço da Ribeira.' *Ocidente*, XV (1941), 297-320.

Comédia sobre a divisa da cidade de Coimbra (1527)

763   See above, nos 315, 354, 366, 675.

Farsa dos almocreves (1527)

764   See above, nos 366, 421.

Tragicomédia pastoril da Serra da Estrêla (1527)

765   See above, no. 675.

Breve sumário da história de Deus (1527)

766   See above, no. 414.

Auto das fadas (1527)

767   Girodon, Jean. 'Le Diable picard de l'*Auto das fadas*.' *BEP*, XIV (1950) 246-70.

768   ——. 'Le Diable picard. Note en marge de l'article de M. Pierre Groult.' *BEP*, XVI (1952), 209-11.
       See following entry.

769   Groult, Pierre. 'Le Diable picard de Gil Vicente.' *BEP*, XVI (1952), 79-95.

770   Hourcade, Pierre. Le Dialecte picard chez Gil Vicente.' *BEP*, XIV (1950), 221-2.
       Introduces the 1950 articles of Teyssier and Girodon, nos 771, 767.

771   Teyssier, Paul. 'Essai d'explication du passage en picard de l'*Auto das fadas* de Gil Vicente.' *BEP*, XIV (1950), 223-45.

O triunfo do Inverno (1529)

772   Frenk Alatorre, Margit. ' "Quien maora ca mi sayo".' *NRFH*, XI (1957), 386-91.

773   Oliveira, Joaquim de. 'A primeira sugestão do mito de Adamastor. Gil Vicente e Luís de Camões: breve estudo comparativo.' *Ocidente*, LXII

(1962), 6-25.
Suggests that Canto V of *Os Lusíadas* was inspired by the *Triunfo do Inverno*.

774   See also above, nos 353, 549, 624.

Jubileu de Amor (1531)

775   Révah, I.S. 'L'Attribution du *Jubilé d'Amours* à Gil Vicente.' *BEP*, XII (1948), 273-8.

Auto da Lusitânia (1532)

776   Aquino, Agostinho de. 'O *Auto da Lusitânia*.' *BGPL*, 4 (January 1966), 28-38.

777   Bopp, Vanda Beatriz. 'O *Auto da Lusitânia*.' *BGPL*, 5 (August 1966), 62-81.

778   Chaves, Luís. 'O *Auto da Lusitânia* de Gil Vicente e o tecelão das mantas d'Alentejo.' *Ocidente*, LVII (1959), 98.

779   See also above, nos 30, 404.

Romagem de agravados (1533)

780   See above, no. 256.

Auto da Cananeia (1534)

781   David, Pierre. 'L'*Auto de la Cananéenne* de Gil Vicente et sa place dans l'année liturgique.' *BEP*, XII (1948), 265-72.

782   Le Gentil, Georges. '*La Cananeia* de Gil Vicente et les mystères français.' *BH*, L (1948), 353-69.

Floresta de enganos (1536)

783   Stathatos, Constantine C. 'Antecedents of Gil Vicente's *Floresta de enganos*.' *L-BR*, IX (1972), 87-95.
Literary and folkloric analogues. Incorporated in the Introduction to his edition of the play (pp. 46-56): see above, no. 169.

784   See also above, no. 669.

Obra da geração humana

785   Révah, I.S. 'La Source de la *Obra da geração humana* et de l'*Auto da Alma*.' *BHTP*, I (1950), 1-32.
Ludolph of Saxony's *Vita Christi*.

786   See also above, no. 286.

Auto de Deus Padre e Justiça e Misericórdia

787   Asensio, Eugenio. 'El soneto "No me mueve, mi Dios . . . " y un auto vicentino inspirados en Santa Catalina de Siena.' *RFE*, XXXIV (1950), 125-36.

788   Martins, Mário. 'As origens do *Auto de Deus Padre e justiça e miseri-córdia.' Lusitania Sacra*, III (1958), 47-66.

789   See also above, no. 286.

On Miscellaneous Works

790*   Pestana, Eduardo Antonino. 'O *Sermão* de Gil Vicente em Abrantes.' *Palestra*, 4 (1959), 34-48.

791   Ricard, Robert. *'Missa seca* chez Gil Vicente.' *Colóquio*, 12 (February 1961), 55-6.
       Using a passage from *Maria Parda* as point of departure, he traces the history of the practice of *missa seca*.

792   Riggio, Edward A. 'The Originality of Gil Vicente's *Maria Parda.' Journal of the American Portuguese Cultural Society*, III (1969), 44-55.

793   Rocha, Andrée Crabbé. 'Duas cartas de Gil Vicente.' *Dionysos*, X, 12 (September 1965), 27-8.
       On the letter which Gil Vicente sent to D. João III from Santarém and on his prologue to the *Copilaçam*.

794   São Payo, Marquês de. 'No rescaldo do centenário vicentino. Como se teria apelidado ao certo Afonso Lopes o Judeu das trovas de Gil Vicente? Çapayo, Çâpayo ou Capayo?' *Armas e Troféus*, VII (1966), 167-9.

795   See also above, nos 353, 357, 359.

INDEX OF SCHOLARS AND TRANSLATORS

Numbers indicate entries. Those preceded by B correspond to entries in the section on Bibliographic Sources. Those preceded by a decimal point refer to reviews. Names incidentally mentioned (e.g. editors of *Festschriften* in which articles on Vicente are published) are excluded from this Index.

SUBJECT INDEX

Numbers indicate entries.